Eco-Warriors On TV Saving Planet Act

Eco-Warriors On TV Saving Planet Act

Rafeal Mechlore

UNIEK ENTERPRISES

CONTENTS

INDEX 1

Introduction 3

Chapter 1 12

Chapter 2 24

Chapter 3 37

Chapter 4 50

Chapter 5 65

Chapter 6 77

Chapter 7 91

INDEX

Introduction

1. Brief overview of the book
2. Importance of environmental activism in the modern world

Chapter 1: The Eco-Warrior Concept
1.1. Defining an eco-warrior
1.2. The evolution of eco-consciousness
1.3. The intersection of reality TV and environmental activism

Chapter 2: The Contestants
2.1. Introduction to the eco-warriors
2.2. Their diverse backgrounds and motivations
2.3. The selection process

Chapter 3: Eco-Challenges
3.1. Description of the eco-challenge format
3.2. Examples of specific challenges
3.3. The importance of eco-education within challenges

Chapter 4: Real-World Impact
4.1. The unique prize: spearheading environmental projects
4.2. Success stories of past winners
4.3. The long-term effects of these projects on communities

Chapter 5: The Behind-the-Scenes
5.1. The making of an eco-warrior reality TV show
5.2. Insights from the show's creators and producers
5.3. The challenges and ethical considerations in producing an eco-conscious show

Chapter 6: The Environmental Issues
6.1. Deep dive into the environmental challenges showcased on the show
6.2. Expert interviews on each issue
6.3. The interconnectedness of these challenges

Chapter 7: The Contestants' Journey
7.1. Personal narratives and transformations
7.2. Lessons learned along the way
7.3. The impact on their lives after the show

Introduction

In a time characterized by the direness of ecological worries, the job of media in molding our aggregate impression of the regular world and the battle to save it has never been more articulated. In the unfurling show of our natural emergency, TV, as a strong medium, has arisen as a strong entertainer in forming how we might interpret ecological issues and our reactions to them. The worldwide stage has seen a significant change in how natural difficulties are outlined, depicted, and, all the more vitally, how they are tended to by an expansive range of "Eco-Heroes" whose stories have been radiated into our lounges through the little screen. It is inside this advancing media scene that we find the intricate and convincing story of "Eco-Champions on television: Saving the Planet Act."

The expression "Eco-Hero" itself has gone through a change over the long run. What was once a periphery assignment has developed into a standard name for people and gatherings devoted to natural activism. These cutting edge heroes bridle the force of TV to communicate their messages and move activity. They range from charming TV characters who host devoted eco-accommodating shows to narrative producers and analytical columnists who utilize the medium to reveal insight into natural mal-treatments. As the planet wrestles with environmental change, territory obliteration, contamination, and a large group of other biological dangers, the job of these Eco-Heroes takes on expanding importance.

TV, as a medium, has the remarkable capacity to connect geological and social partitions. It interfaces individuals from various corners of the world, carrying them nearer to the marvels of our planet and the difficulties it faces. Natural issues, once restricted to scholastic talk and specialty narratives, have now entered the standard through the open and vivid mechanism of TV. This progress mirrors a change in cultural mindfulness, one that perceives the squeezing need to draw in with these difficulties on a more extensive scale. "Eco-Champions on television" investigates how this progress has unfurled and the central members who have driven the charge.

The demonstration of "Saving the Planet," as suggested by the title of this story, infers an aggregate liability. The actual term highlights the common perspective that ecological insurance is a widespread pursuit, rising above political, social, and topographical limits. It is a presentation, a demonstration that is communicated to a worldwide crowd, and a show unfurls continuously as the actual stage — the Earth — stands up to expanding risk. The illustration of an "act" points out the performative part of ecological activism on TV. While the responsibility of Eco-Champions is veritable, it is likewise a type of theater, a painstakingly arranged story introduced to watchers in a manner that is both connecting with and effective.

This story investigates the nuanced exchange between natural activism and the mode of TV. It dives into the inspirations, difficulties, and triumphs of the individuals who have made it their central goal to be the Eco-Champions on the little screen. It additionally looks at the power elements at play, the methodologies utilized, and the impact that TV holds in molding how we might interpret the normal world. This story, at its center, is an assessment of the convergence between the natural emergency and the vehicle of TV, and the focal characters in this unfurling show.

The ascent of Eco-Heroes on TV has not happened in confinement. It is important for a more extensive account — an account of ecological arousing and expanding public mindfulness. As the outcomes of natural debasement become more evident and prompt, so too does the significance of drawing in with these issues. TV, with its unrivaled reach and impact, fills in as both a mirror mirroring our influencing world and an impetus for extraordinary activity. This unique transaction among media and the climate is at the core of our investigation.

The introduction of ecological cognizance on TV can be followed back to when the actual medium was in its outset. While nature narratives had existed for quite a long time, it was only after the late twentieth century that ecological issues got some decent momentum on TV. Programs like "The Undersea Universe of Jacques Cousteau" and "The Shared of Omaha's Wild Realm" brought the miracles of the regular world into the homes of millions, enrapturing crowds with the magnificence and intricacy of the World's environments.

In the years that followed, the natural development got comfortable with its on TV through noticeable figures like David Attenborough. His series, including "The Blue Planet" and "Planet Earth," caught the creative mind of watchers around the world, cultivating a profound appreciation for the planet's biodiversity. These projects denoted a critical change in how TV depicted the climate. Never again was it restricted to the outskirts of diversion; it turned into a subject of focal significance. Attenborough's calming portrayal and stunning visuals transformed environmental-ism into a hypnotizing scene.

TV, as a medium, has an ability to interest to get close to home reactions. It can cause us to feel a significant association with the regular world, and it can likewise incite an instinctive response to ecological obliteration. For some, these close to home associations have prodded them right into it. They have become Eco-Champions of an alternate sort, battling for the planet as well as for the hearts and brains of their kinsmen.

The turn of the 21st century denoted a critical change in the manner ecological issues were covered on TV. As of now not bound to the domain of untamed life narratives and investigation, natural reporting took on a more insightful and fierce tone. This shift was exemplified by Al Carnage's "A Badly designed Truth," an earth shattering narrative that brought the real factors of environmental change to the very front of public talk. Gore, a previous VP of the US, introduced the mounting proof of an Earth-wide temperature boost in a convincing and pressing way. The narrative filled in as a reminder for some, igniting a worldwide discussion on the climate.

As the earnestness of natural issues kept on mounting, TV assumed a basic part in dispersing data and moving activity. The new type of Eco-Heroes on television were not generally restricted to naturalists and pioneers; they included researchers, activists, and standard people who had volunteered to have an effect. TV, through unscripted TV dramas and insightful reporting, gave a stage to these Eco-Fighters to draw in with people in general in a more straightforward and quick manner.

One such model is the stunningly famous reality series "Survivor." While the show is principally known for its serious difficulties and social elements, it has likewise integrated topics of ecological maintainability. Competitors are in many cases set in remote and testing common habitats, featuring the need to adjust and save these environments. "Survivor" engaged millions as well as incited watchers to think about the delicacy and significance of the regular world.

At the crossing point of TV and environmentalism, the figure of the "Eco-Fighter" started to advance. These people were not limited by a solitary definition. They could be researchers working in the field, activists challenging biological treacheries, or TV has utilizing their foundation to advocate for change. While some centered around bringing issues to light and rousing individual activity, others adopted a more fierce strategy, effectively testing damaging businesses and practices. This diverse portrayal of Eco-Champions on television exhibits the intricacy of their parts in the natural development.

One Eco-Hero who arose as a noticeable figure in this developing story was Bill Nye, the "Science Fellow." Nye, with his instructive TV program, "Bill Nye the Science Fellow," utilized humor and drawing in exhibits to show watchers logical ideas, including those connected with the climate. Nye's receptive and engaging style made complex points open to an expansive crowd, and his show turned into a staple in numerous study halls. Through the force of TV, Nye taught and roused endless people to foster an interest in science and natural issues.

As TV kept on developing, it embraced new configurations and types that considered a more unique investigation of ecological worries. Unscripted tv programs like "The Astonishing Race" and "The Eco-Challenge" integrated natural difficulties and undertakings into their storylines. Contenders were frequently expected to draw in with nature in manners that stressed the significance of environmental obligation.

In lined up with these turns of events, natural narratives acquired another unmistakable quality on TV. Works like "A Badly designed Truth" were trailed by Michael Moore's "Fahrenheit 9/11," which evaluated the Shrubbery organization's arrangements and their natural ramifications. These narratives showed the way that TV could act as a stage for difference and backing, permitting producers to impart strong messages to a worldwide crowd.

The defining moment in the Eco-Heroes story, be that as it may, showed up with the multiplication of committed eco-accommodating shows. TV stations perceived the developing interest in natural issues and started to foster projects that were focused on maintainability, protection, and activism. One of the most famous of these shows was "The Crocodile Tracker," facilitated by the energetic Steve Irwin. Irwin's extraordinary mix of instruction, protection, and diversion caught the minds of watchers all over the planet. He changed from an animal specialist and natural life.

1. **Brief overview of the book**

   "Eco-Champions on television: Saving the Planet Act" is a convincing investigation of the complex and developing connection among TV and natural activism. This story dives into the complex universe of Eco-Champions, the people and gatherings committed to bringing issues to light and battling for the conservation of our planet, and how they influence the force of TV to do as such. In reality as we know it where ecological difficulties have become progressively squeezing, the impact of TV as a mechanism for natural narrating has never been more critical.

   The story leaves on an excursion through time, following the underlying foundations of ecological cognizance on TV and its development into a useful asset for bringing issues to light and prompting activity. It looks at the essential jobs played by conspicuous figures like David Attenborough, Steve Irwin, Bill Nye, and Al Butchery, who changed the medium into a stage for ecological instruction and support. These people taught watchers about the regular world as well as caught their hearts and psyches, driving them to check out protection and manageability.

   The book recognizes that TV has the extraordinary capacity to rise above geological and social limits, making it a widespread stage for resolving ecological issues. As the planet wrestles with environmental change, natural surroundings obliteration, contamination, and a scope of biological dangers, TV has turned into the medium through which these emergencies are outlined, depicted, and eventually tended to. The demonstration of "Saving the Planet" is outlined as an aggregate liability, a continuous exhibition that unfurls progressively as our Earth faces expanding hazard. This account investigates how TV shapes the view of natural issues and how Eco-Fighters on television are crucial entertainers in this unfurling show.

The book features the job of natural schooling and motivation, causing to notice the way that TV has the ability to draw in watchers on a significant profound level. Whether through amazing visuals of unblemished scenes or deplorable depictions of ecological debasement, TV has the ability to make profound associations between the crowd and the normal world. These associations, thusly, drive watchers to make a move, become all the more earth cognizant, and add to the safeguarding of the planet.

Besides, the book perceives the transaction among media and environmentalism, delineating how TV has the ability to refine natural issues, making them interesting and spurring watchers to have an effect. Ecological worries, once restricted to scholastic circles and specialty narratives, are currently important for the standard discussion, thanks by and large to the vehicle of TV. This account investigates the manners by which TV has demystified biological issues, separating them into justifiable stories available to individuals of all foundations and ages.

The book likewise recognizes that Eco-Fighters on television come in different structures and are not limited by a solitary definition. They can be researchers leading field research, activists fighting biological treacheries, or TV has utilizing their foundation to advocate for change. This complex portrayal of Eco-Fighters on television features the variety of approaches taken in the natural development. A few spotlight on bringing issues to light and motivating individual activity, while others embrace a more fierce methodology, effectively testing horrendous businesses and practices.

As the story unfurls, obviously the ascent of Eco-Champions on TV is important for a more extensive account — a natural arousing and expanding public mindfulness. The mechanism of TV assumes an essential part in this enlivening, associating individuals from various corners of the world and carrying them nearer to the marvels of our planet and the difficulties it faces. As TV keeps on advancing, Eco-Fighters assume a fundamental part in tending to new and arising natural difficulties, from the effects of man-made consciousness and computerization to the outcomes of overconsumption and waste.

The book likewise addresses the changing scene of TV and media in the advanced age. While TV stays an amazing asset for narrating, the web and virtual entertainment stages have changed the manner in which Eco-Fighters draw in with their crowds. These computerized stages offer an additional intelligent and quick method for correspondence, empowering continuous updates, commitment with watchers, and the preparation of huge scope natural developments. The cutting edge Eco-Fighter frequently utilizes a multi-stage approach, utilizing TV close by computerized media to make a thorough effect.

Additionally, the book recognizes the reactions and difficulties that accompany the job of TV in ecological activism. Some contend that TV misrepresents complex ecological issues, transforming them into sensationalized and diversion driven stories. There is worry that the emphasis on alluring hosts and exciting visuals can eclipse the gravity of the difficulties within reach, possibly prompting shallow commitment with basic issues. The book perceives that there is a scarcely discernible difference that Eco-Champions on television should step, exploring the strain among promotion and diversion, truth and display.

Moreover, the book features worries about portrayal and inclusivity in the ecological development. It questions who will be an Eco-Champion on TV and whether certain voices and viewpoints are advantaged over others. As the medium develops, there is a developing acknowledgment of the requirement for variety and inclusivity inside the natural development. This acknowledgment stretches out to both the substance and the people who address it. Natural difficulties excessively influence minimized networks, and it is basic that their voices are heard and their accounts told on TV.

The business idea of TV presents another test, as the quest for high viewership can once in a while prompt trade offs in the genuineness of the ecological message. The book recognizes the fragile difficult exercise that Eco-Champions on television should explore, attempting to catch consideration and rouse activity without neglecting to focus on the profundity and intricacy of natural issues. TV is a two sided deal, offering the potential for both significant effect and minimization.

All in all, "Eco-Heroes on television: Saving the Planet Act" is an exhaustive investigation of the transaction among TV and natural activism. It follows the development of natural cognizance on TV, perceiving the essential jobs played by conspicuous figures and the change of the medium into a stage for ecological schooling and backing. The book highlights the close to home force of TV, its capacity to make associations among watchers and the regular world, and its job in acculturating natural issues.

Also, the account praises the complex idea of Eco-Champions on television, recognizing the assorted methodologies taken in the natural development. It features the changing scene of TV and media in the computerized age, where Eco-Fighters frequently utilize a multi-stage way to deal with expand their effect. The book perceives the reactions and difficulties that accompany the job of TV in ecological activism, from misrepresentation to worries about portrayal and inclusivity.

The demonstration of "Saving the Planet" stays an aggregate liability, and TV keeps on being a strong stage where this exhibition unfurls. The story fills in as a demonstration of the force of narrating and the potential for change, advising us that, notwithstanding squeezing natural difficulties, the demonstrations of Eco-Fighters in the fantastic story of "Saving the Planet Act" are more imperative than any other time.

2. Importance of environmental activism in the modern world

The significance of ecological activism in the advanced world couldn't possibly be more significant. As we explore the difficulties of the 21st hundred years, our planet faces a scope of squeezing biological issues that compromise the prosperity of both current and people in the future. Natural activism assumes a focal part in tending to these difficulties, bringing issues to light, and driving change. In this conversation, we will dig into the meaning of natural activism in our contemporary setting, underlining its effect on worldwide maintainability, human wellbeing, biodiversity, and the general personal satisfaction.

Worldwide Manageability:

Natural activism is inseparably connected to worldwide supportability. At the core of manageability lies the idea of addressing the necessities of the present without compromising the capacity of people in the future to address their own issues. In our current reality where asset consumption, environmental change, and overconsumption are conspicuous worries, natural activism fills in as a basic power in advancing economical practices.

Activists and associations work to battle rehearses that exhaust limited assets, like petroleum products, and champion inexhaustible and clean energy choices. They advocate for mindful utilization and creation designs that guarantee assets are utilized proficiently and morally. Additionally, they challenge the folly of strategies that focus on quick monetary increases to the detriment of long haul natural soundness. In doing as such, ecological activism adds to the conservation of a planet equipped for supporting life for a long time into the future.

Human Wellbeing:

Ecological activism significantly affects human wellbeing. The corruption of the climate, contamination, and openness to harmful substances present critical dangers to human prosperity. Air and water contamination, for example, can prompt an extensive variety of medical problems, from respiratory infections to different types of disease.

Activists advocate for clean air and clean water, pushing for stricter ecological guidelines and industry responsibility. By attempting to diminish contamination and natural poisons, they endeavor to make better everyday environments for networks around the world. Besides, through drives that advance economical horticulture and safe food rehearses, natural activists address the essential association between ecological wellbeing and the prosperity of individuals.

Biodiversity Preservation:

The variety of life on The planet, from plants and creatures to microorganisms, is essential to the working of environments and the general strength of our planet. In any case, the cutting edge world has seen a quick decrease in biodiversity because of environment obliteration, contamination, environmental change, and the presentation of obtrusive species.

Ecological activism assumes an imperative part in upholding for the security and preservation of biodiversity. Moderates and activists work to lay out safeguarded regions, take part in natural surroundings rebuilding, and backing endeavors to battle unlawful untamed life exchange. Through their work, they try to protect individual species as well as the many-sided trap of connections that supports life on The planet.

Environmental Change Moderation:

One of the most dire ecological difficulties within recent memory is environmental change. The consuming of petroleum products, deforestation, and other human exercises have prompted a sensational expansion in ozone depleting substance outflows, bringing about climbing worldwide temperatures, ocean level ascent, and more continuous outrageous climate occasions.

Natural activists have been at the front of endeavors to moderate environmental change. They advocate for approaches and activities that lessen fossil fuel byproducts, progress to environmentally friendly power sources, and advance energy productivity. Their work, for example, supporting worldwide environment arrangements like the Paris Understanding, shows the worldwide reach and effect of ecological activism in tending to this existential danger.

Personal satisfaction and Civil rights:

Natural activism is intrinsically connected to the personal satisfaction and civil rights. Natural debasement frequently lopsidedly influences underestimated and weak networks, prompting ecological shameful acts. For instance, low-pay networks are bound to be situated close to wellsprings of contamination and are, thusly, at more serious gamble of unfavorable wellbeing impacts.

Natural activists champion ecological equity, taking a stab at evenhanded admittance to clean air, water, and a protected living climate for all. They challenge ecological prejudice and unjust circulation of natural weights. In doing as such, they make progress toward making a more pleasant and all the more society where the advantages of a perfect and sound climate are shared by all.

Impacting Strategy and Regulation:

Natural activists assume a basic part in forming strategy and regulation at nearby, public, and worldwide levels. Their promotion and strain on legislatures and organizations can prompt the execution of guidelines that safeguard the climate and human wellbeing. They likewise go about as guard dogs, considering legislatures and companies responsible for their activities and guaranteeing that they stick to ecological guidelines.

Outstanding triumphs of natural activism incorporate the section of regulations like the Perfect Air Act and Clean Water Act in the US, as well as peaceful accords like the Montreal Convention, which means to safeguard the ozone layer. The effect of these regulative triumphs reaches out a long ways past the dissident local area, decidedly influencing society in general.

Bringing issues to light and Motivating Activity:

Ecological activism fills in as a strong vehicle for bringing issues to light and moving activity on natural issues. Through different means, including fights, instructive missions, narratives, and online entertainment, activists point out basic biological difficulties. They make sense of the results of ecological debasement in engaging terms and proposition arrangements that people and networks can execute.

By making natural issues more available and connecting with, ecological activists urge people to get a sense of ownership with their environmental impression. This strengthening prompts boundless changes in conduct, including taking on reasonable works on, supporting eco-accommodating items and administrations, and partaking in nearby natural drives.

Worldwide Cooperation:

Natural activism is a worldwide development that encourages coordinated effort and fortitude among individuals and associations from various regions of the planet. Natural activists frequently cooperate to resolve gives that rise above public boundaries, for example, environmental change, deforestation, and sea protection.

Worldwide organizations and unions, for example, Greenpeace and the World Untamed life Asset, embody the force of worldwide joint effort. These associations influence their aggregate solidarity to impact worldwide approaches, advocate for natural security, and assemble assets for protection endeavors. The interconnectedness of ecological issues requests an organized worldwide reaction, and natural activism fills in as a binding together power in this undertaking.

Supporting Reasonable Economies:

Ecological activism perceives the connection between a solid climate and a feasible economy. Feasible practices, like sustainable power, preservation, and dependable asset the board, safeguard the climate as well as advance monetary solidness and occupation creation.

Activists work to change social orders toward reasonable, round economies that limit squander and diminish the natural impression. Thusly, they support financial frameworks that are less reliant upon limited assets and stronger even with natural difficulties.

Encouraging Development and Innovative Progressions:

Natural activism drives development and innovative progressions that can address ecological difficulties. The earnestness of these issues has prodded innovative work in regions like clean energy advances, squander decrease, and practical agribusiness.

Developments, from electric vehicles to effective reusing strategies, have been moved by the need to address natural worries. Ecological activists frequently team up with researchers, designers, and business visionaries to carry these advancements to the front line and supporter for their far and wide reception.

Chapter 1

The Eco-Warrior Concept

The idea of the "Eco-Fighter" addresses a strong and complex model in the continuous story of environmentalism. These people and gatherings, frequently energetic, devoted, and strong, have arisen as heroes of the regular world. The expression "Eco-Champion" epitomizes a different scope of natural activists and supporters who have taken up the reason for environmental conservation and maintainability. In this investigation, we dig into the pith of the Eco-Fighter idea, analyzing its starting points, development, and persevering through importance in the cutting edge world.

Beginnings of the Eco-Hero Idea:

The starting points of the Eco-Hero idea can be followed back to the natural developments of the twentieth 100 years. It was while developing ecological mindfulness prompted another rush of activists and progressives. The expression "Eco-Fighter" arose as an image of their devotion and assurance to safeguard the climate. These early Eco-Fighters frequently centered around issues like wild preservation, untamed life insurance, and hostile to contamination endeavors.

Figures like Rachel Carson, whose noteworthy book "Quiet Spring" brought issues to light about the risks of pesticides, can be viewed as the absolute earliest Eco-Heroes. Her work, alongside that of different naturalists like John Muir, Aldo Leopold, and David Brower, established the groundwork for the advanced ecological development. Their endeavors to save normal spaces, protect jeopardized species, and challenge unsafe modern practices set up for another age of Eco-Fighters.

The Development of the Eco-Hero:

After some time, the Eco-Hero idea developed to include a more extensive scope of natural issues and approaches. While early natural activism frequently centered around unambiguous areas of concern, for example, untamed life preservation or living space insurance, present day Eco-Heroes draw in with an expansive range of biological difficulties. These difficulties incorporate environmental change, living space obliteration, deforestation, contamination, overconsumption, and a large group of other interconnected issues.

The advancement of the Eco-Fighter idea additionally reflects changes in the media scene. While early activists depended on printed materials and grassroots getting sorted out, contemporary Eco-Heroes bridle the force of advanced media and social stages to assemble worldwide crowds. This advancement has extended the scope and effect of their promotion endeavors, empowering them to associate with people and networks around the world.

Variety of Eco-Heroes:

The Eco-Fighter idea embraces variety in the two its defenders and approaches. Eco-Champions are not restricted to a particular segment or calling; they come from varying backgrounds. They can be researchers directing fundamental exploration, activists driving fights and missions, writers examining natural maltreatments, policymakers upholding for authoritative change, or teachers advancing eco-accommodating practices. They are people and associations who share a typical obligation to safeguarding the climate.

In addition, the idea of the Eco-Hero rises above geographic limits. Natural activists can be tracked down in all edges of the globe, upholding for issues applicable to their districts. Their aggregate endeavors stand out enough to be noticed to neighborhood, public, and worldwide natural worries, stressing the interconnectedness of environmental difficulties.

The Inspiration of Eco-Champions:

The inspiration of Eco-Champions is established from a profound perspective of obligation to the normal world and people in the future. They are driven by an energy for ecological security and a significant comprehension of the results of inaction. The inspiration frequently rises out of a craving to guarantee that the planet's assets and biodiversity are protected for people in the future to appreciate.

Eco-Fighters draw motivation from their association with the climate. Many have individual accounts of encountering the excellence of the regular world, whether through youth encounters in nature or through their own examination and investigation. This association powers their assurance to go up against ecological difficulties and drive positive change.

Drawing in with Ecological Issues:

Eco-Heroes draw in with natural issues in different ways, and their methodologies can be comprehensively classified into two principal techniques: backing and activity.

Backing: Promotion arranged Eco-Champions utilize their voices and stages to bring issues to light about natural worries. They frequently influence the force of narrating, whether through composition, public talking, or media appearances, to convey the desperation of biological difficulties. Through support, they expect to impact general assessment, shape strategy, and drive change through mindfulness and schooling.

Activity: Activity situated Eco-Fighters adopt an additional involved strategy to environmentalism. They effectively partake in endeavors to resolve explicit issues, for example, taking part in fights, taking part in ecological reclamation projects, directing logical exploration, or driving preservation drives. Their work frequently includes direct cooperation with the climate, whether in the field, adrift, or in research centers.

The Media and the Eco-Fighter Idea:

The job of media in forming and sustaining the Eco-Champion idea is huge. Media stages, going from customary papers and TV to current computerized and online entertainment, have been instrumental in enhancing the voices of Eco-Heroes and carrying their messages to a more extensive crowd. Natural narratives, analytical newscasting, and eco-accommodating TV programs have all added to the advancement of the Eco-Champion prime example.

TV, specifically, plays had an essential impact in introducing the Eco-Hero idea to a worldwide crowd. Shows that attention on ecological issues, for example, "Planet Earth" or "The Blue Planet," have taught watchers about the normal world as well as raised the situation with natural activists. TV characters like David Attenborough and Steve Irwin, who consolidated schooling, diversion, and promotion, have become famous figures in the Eco-Champion account.

In the computerized age, the scope of the Eco-Fighter idea has extended further, because of the web and virtual entertainment. Activists and associations use these stages to share data, prepare support, and draw in with a different worldwide crowd. Online entertainment, specifically, has considered more quick and intuitive correspondence, empowering Eco-Champions to interface with similar people and rally support for their causes.

Eco-Champions in Mainstream society:

Eco-Champions have had a massive effect in mainstream society, with their accounts and activities moving endless people. The model has been depicted in writing, film, and workmanship, further hardening its position in the public creative mind. Characters in books, narratives, and component films frequently exemplify the soul of the Eco-Hero, exhibiting their energy, responsibility, and the difficulties they face in their mission to safeguard the climate.

While certain portrayals in mainstream society can romanticize the job of the Eco-Fighter, they additionally shed light on the fundamental work these people do and the penances they make. This depiction builds up the thought that natural activism isn't just an individual calling yet a basic commitment to everyone's benefit.

Difficulties and Reactions:

The Eco-Fighter idea isn't without its difficulties and reactions. While ecological activism is fundamental, it has confronted examination and resistance from different quarters. Pundits contend that some Eco-Champions might distort complex natural issues or resort to sentimentality to gather consideration. They battle that this approach can prompt a shallow comprehension of the main concerns and prevent helpful discourse.

There are likewise worries about the commodification of environmentalism, where a few Eco-Champions and associations might focus on raising money and marking over real promotion and activity. This commercialization can, now and again, reduce the legitimacy of the ecological message.

Also, the Eco-Hero idea has been related with fierce and revolutionary activities, for example, eco-psychological oppression. While these activities are not agent of the more extensive natural development, they definitely stand out and brought up issues about the morals of specific strategies.

The subject of portrayal and variety inside the Eco-Fighter idea has additionally come to the front. Pundits contend that the model has frequently been related with white, Western figures, which might avoid the voices and viewpoints of underestimated networks, who are excessively impacted by natural difficulties.

The Getting through Meaning of the Eco-Fighter:

Notwithstanding these difficulties and reactions, the Eco-Fighter idea stays huge and persevering. The commitment, strength, and energy of Eco-Champions keep on driving advancement in the natural development. They go about as impetuses for change, activating networks and legislatures to address squeezing natural difficulties. Their work brings issues to light, shapes strategy, motivates activity, and cultivates a feeling of shared liability regarding the planet.

In a world confronting progressively dire natural dangers, the Eco-Champion idea exemplifies the soul of dynamic commitment with biological issues. It fills in as an update that people and gatherings can have an effect and that the security of the climate is an aggregate exertion. The model mirrors the advancement of ecological activism and the assorted methodologies taken to address the intricate and interconnected difficulties within recent memory.

1.1. Defining an eco-warrior

Characterizing an Eco-Hero is a complex undertaking, as the idea encapsulates a different scope of people, gatherings, and approaches devoted to natural promotion and activity. An Eco-Fighter is definitely not a solitary, static model but instead a powerful portrayal of the people who effectively draw in with natural issues and endeavor to safeguard the planet. To extensively characterize an Eco-Fighter, we should investigate their key attributes, inspirations, jobs, and the advancing idea of their work with regards to contemporary natural difficulties.

Key Qualities of an Eco-Champion:

Enthusiasm and Devotion: An Eco-Champion is portrayed by a profound energy for the climate and a committed obligation to its security. They are many times driven by a significant feeling of obligation to defend the normal world.

Promotion: Eco-Champions advocate for natural causes, bringing issues to light about environmental difficulties and supporting for strategy changes. They utilize their voices and stages to impact general assessment and shape the talk on ecological issues.

Activity Situated: While backing is a fundamental part of being an Eco-Champion, they are likewise activity arranged. They take part in active endeavors to resolve natural issues, like taking an interest in fights, driving protection drives, or directing logical exploration.

Multidisciplinary Approach: Eco-Champions frequently embrace a multidisciplinary approach, drawing from fields like science, strategy, instruction, and backing. This variety of skill permits them to address a large number of ecological issues.

Versatility: Eco-Heroes are known for their strength even with natural difficulties and difficulty. They persevere in their endeavors to safeguard the climate, in any event, when confronted with hindrances and mishaps.

Worldwide Point of view: Numerous Eco-Fighters embrace a worldwide point of view, perceiving the interconnectedness of natural issues across borders. They team up with people and associations overall to address shared difficulties.

Moral Stewardship: Eco-Heroes frequently view themselves as moral stewards of the climate, driven by a longing to guarantee that the planet's assets and biodiversity are saved for people in the future.

Inspirations of an Eco-Hero:

Eco-Heroes are persuaded by various elements that drive their obligation to natural promotion and activity:

Association with the Climate: Numerous Eco-Heroes have a unique interaction to the climate, frequently established in youth encounters, significant minutes in nature, or a profound love for the normal world. This association powers their craving to safeguard it.

Feeling of obligation: An inborn feeling of obligation to people in the future is a strong inspiration. Eco-Champions feel liable for guaranteeing that the planet's assets and environments are passed down unblemished to the individuals who come after them.

Figuring out Results: They have a significant comprehension of the results of natural debasement, perceiving the biological, social, and monetary effects of inaction.

Motivation and Trust: Eco-Fighters are roused by the potential for positive change. They accept that by making a move, they can add to a more brilliant, more feasible future for all.

Jobs of an Eco-Hero:

Eco-Heroes take on various jobs in the field of natural promotion and activity, mirroring their assorted methodologies and subject matters:

Advocate: Promotion is a focal job for some Eco-Fighters. They utilize their voices and stages to bring issues to light about natural issues, impact strategy, and prepare support for protection endeavors.

Researcher and Specialist: Some Eco-Heroes are researchers and scientists who direct examinations and examinations to more readily figure out natural difficulties.

Their work adds to the group of information that illuminates natural approach and direction.

Teacher: Eco-Champions frequently act as instructors, granting information about natural issues and maintainability to people and networks. They work to rouse activity by illuminating and connecting with the general population.

Extremist: Lobbyist Eco-Heroes are known for their dynamic commitment to fights, crusades, and direct activity. They utilize their enthusiasm and assurance to challenge earth damaging practices and supporter for change.

Traditionalist: Numerous Eco-Fighters are moderates who center around saving and safeguarding regular territories, jeopardized species, and biodiversity. Their work frequently includes living space rebuilding, reforestation, and natural life security.

Strategy Backer: Eco-Champions who fill in as strategy advocates impact natural arrangements at nearby, public, and global levels. They draw in with officials, government organizations, and worldwide bodies to shape regulation that safeguards the climate.

Media and Specialized Subject matter expert: The media assumes a vital part in molding natural mindfulness, and Eco-Heroes working in media and correspondence spend significant time in scattering data and narrating about environmental difficulties.

The Developing Idea of Eco-Champion Work:

Crafted by an Eco-Champion has developed because of the changing natural scene and headways in innovation and media:

Advanced Media: The ascent of computerized media and social stages has extended the compass of Eco-Heroes, permitting them to associate with worldwide crowds, prepare backing, and offer data continuously.

Worldwide Joint effort: Eco-Fighters progressively team up on a worldwide scale to resolve natural issues that rise above public boundaries, for example, environmental change, deforestation, and sea preservation. Worldwide organizations and unions enhance their aggregate effect.

Various Natural Issues: Current Eco-Heroes address an expansive range of biological difficulties, from environmental change and territory obliteration to contamination and overconsumption. They perceive the interconnected idea of these issues and endeavor to comprehensively handle them.

Portrayal and Inclusivity: There is a developing acknowledgment of the requirement for variety and inclusivity inside the ecological development. Eco-Heroes work to guarantee that the voices of minimized networks, who are in many cases lopsidedly impacted by natural difficulties, are heard and addressed.

Adjusting Backing and Activity: Eco-Champions explore the test of adjusting support and activity, as well as the pressure among mindfulness and misrepresentation. They endeavor to draw in with ecological issues exhaustively and legitimately.

Commercialization and Morals: Eco-Fighters are careful about the likely commercialization of environmentalism, guaranteeing that the validness of the natural message isn't undermined by raising money and marking.

1.2. The evolution of eco-consciousness

The development of eco-cognizance addresses a huge change in human mindfulness and values concerning the climate and our job in saving it. Over the long haul, the idea of eco-cognizance has developed from an undeveloped comprehension of the normal world to a more modern, interconnected, and pressing familiarity with natural issues. This advancement is set apart by unmistakable stages, each molded by cultural, logical, innovative, and social movements. In this investigation, we follow the improvement of eco-cognizance and its significant ramifications for how we see and address natural difficulties.

Beginnings of Eco-Cognizance:

Eco-cognizance has its foundations in the early philosophical, otherworldly, and social convictions of native social orders and customary societies. These social orders frequently held profound adoration for the normal world, seeing it as hallowed and indispensable to their lives. The interconnectedness of nature and humankind was an essential piece of their conviction frameworks, encouraging a feeling of obligation toward the climate.

Numerous native networks rehearsed feasible land use and asset the executives, showing an early type of eco-cognizance. This amicable relationship with nature was based on standards of correspondence and stewardship, where people took from the land yet additionally offered back through customs, practices, and functions.

The Modern Insurgency and the Development of Ecological Worries:

The beginning of the Modern Upheaval in the late eighteenth century denoted a critical defining moment in the development of eco-cognizance. Fast industrialization achieved uncommon urbanization, mechanical progressions, and financial development. Nonetheless, it likewise prompted natural debasement for an enormous scope.

As metropolitan focuses extended and businesses blast, issues like air and water contamination, deforestation, and living space annihilation turned out to be progressively evident. The unfavorable natural effects of industrialization raised worries among a developing number of scholars and activists. Environmentalism, as a reaction to these worries, started to arise.

Preservation Developments and the Introduction of Current Environmentalism:

The late nineteenth and mid twentieth hundreds of years saw the introduction of preservation developments, driven by conspicuous figures like John Muir, Theodore Roosevelt, and Gifford Pinchot. These people supported for the safeguarding of regular scenes, the foundation of public parks, and the practical administration of assets. Their endeavors denoted the change from conventional types of eco-awareness to more formalized and strategy arranged environmentalism.

The preservation developments established the groundwork for present day environmentalism, accentuating the significance of safeguarding normal magnificence and biodiversity for people in the future. These early traditionalists perceived the characteristic worth of nature and made way for more extensive cultural changes in contemplating the climate.

Natural Arousing during the 1960s and 1970s:

The 1960s and 1970s were groundbreaking a long time for eco-cognizance. A progression of occasions and distributions prompted an increased public consciousness of natural issues. Remarkable among these occasions was the distribution of Rachel Carson's "Quiet Spring" in 1962, which uncovered the adverse impacts of pesticides and electrifies public worry about natural wellbeing.

All the while, the primary Earth Day in 1970, which affected great many individuals in the US and all over the planet, denoted a critical stage in the development of eco-cognizance. It represented the force of aggregate activity in resolving natural issues and prodded the death of key ecological regulation, including the Perfect Air Act and the Spotless Water Act.

The 1970s additionally saw the establishing of ecological associations, for example, Greenpeace and the Normal Assets Guard Gathering, further solidifying the job of coordinated activism in eco-cognizance.

Eco-Awareness and the Mainstreaming of Natural Worries:

The 1980s and 1990s saw the mainstreaming of eco-awareness. Natural worries became essential to political and public talk, with legislatures and companies progressively perceiving the significance of resolving biological issues.

Peaceful accords and culminations, remembering the Unified Countries System Show for Environmental Change and the Rio Earth Highest point, carried ecological issues to the worldwide stage. Environmental change, biodiversity misfortune, and reasonable advancement became focal subjects of conversation, building up the earnestness of tending to these difficulties.

All the while, media outlets assumed a huge part in molding eco-cognizance. Narratives like "A Badly arranged Truth" and nature projects, for example, "Planet Earth" dazzled crowds, expanding familiarity with ecological issues and rousing activity.

Mechanical Progressions and Eco-Cognizant Advancements:

The 21st century has seen the ascent of creative advances and approaches that have supported eco-cognizance. Clean energy innovations, headways in reusing and squander decrease, and the multiplication of feasible transportation choices have become key to tending to ecological worries.

The advanced age has likewise empowered far and wide mindfulness and activism. Web-based entertainment and online stages have permitted people and associations to interface, prepare, and share data on a worldwide scale. Issues that might have once slipped by everyone's notice are presently brought to the front of public cognizance through viral missions and online petitions.

Eco-Awareness and the Anthropocene:

The idea of the Anthropocene, signifying the ongoing land age portrayed by human impact in the world, highlights the meaning of eco-cognizance in the cutting edge period. This new age perceives humankind's job in molding the climate, from environmental change to biodiversity misfortune. Eco-cognizance is, to some extent, a reaction to this acknowledgment, as society wrestles with the significant ramifications of our activities on the World's frameworks.

As eco-cognizance develops, there is a developing comprehension that people and social orders should expect a more capable and practical job in molding the Anthropocene. This includes diminishing fossil fuel byproducts, saving normal environments, and embracing roundabout economies that limit waste and asset utilization.

Difficulties and Contemplations in Eco-Awareness:

While eco-cognizance has made some amazing progress, it actually faces huge difficulties:

Conduct Change: Moving human way of behaving to line up with eco-cognizant qualities stays a mind boggling challenge. Defeating latency and working on well established propensities are critical obstacles.

Financial Interests: Monetary interests frequently struggle with eco-cognizant drives. The change to additional maintainable practices might be seen as exorbitant, influencing businesses, occupations, and benefits.

Inclusivity and Equity: Guaranteeing that eco-cognizance is comprehensive and simply is vital. Minimized people group are in many cases lopsidedly impacted by natural issues, and tending to this imbalance is a fundamental piece of eco-awareness.

Political Will: The political will to order significant ecological approaches shifts universally. Numerous nations are attempting to offset monetary development with natural manageability.

The Continuous Advancement of Eco-Awareness:

Eco-awareness keeps on developing because of arising natural difficulties. Environmental change, living space misfortune, contamination, and the conservation of biodiversity are focal issues driving the development of eco-awareness. Furthermore, the acknowledgment of the interconnection between biological, financial, and social frameworks has prompted more all encompassing ways to deal with resolving ecological issues.

The development of grassroots developments, youth-drove activism, and the job of native information frameworks in protection and supportability mirror the advancing idea of eco-cognizance. These developments underscore the criticalness of making a move and the requirement for an exhaustive way to deal with ecological difficulties.

The future of eco-awareness lies in the possession of people, networks, states, and associations around the world. A unique idea will proceed to adjust and extend as society wrestles with the perplexing and interconnected natural issues within recent memory.

1.3. The intersection of reality TV and environmental activism

The convergence of unscripted television and natural activism addresses a dynamic and powerful cooperative energy between two apparently different universes. Unscripted television, described by its unscripted and frequently emotional substance, has acquired colossal notoriety throughout recent many years. At the same time, natural activism has become progressively huge as the world wrestles with earnest biological difficulties. The combination of these two domains has led to a one of a kind stage for raising ecological mindfulness, rousing activity, and catalyzing change. In this investigation, we dive into the significant effect and multi-layered nature of the crossing point of unscripted television and ecological activism.

The Ubiquity and Impact of Unscripted television:

Unscripted television has turned into a worldwide peculiarity, spellbinding crowds with a wide cluster of content, from ability contests like "American Icon" and "The X Variable" to docuseries, for example, "The Genuine Housewives" and "Survivor." The class' allure lies in its unscripted, eccentric, and engaging nature, which offers watchers a voyeuristic look into the lives, difficulties, and wins of the members.

Unscripted television impacts mainstream society, molding patterns, presenting essential characters, and frequently filling in as a mirror reflecting cultural qualities and ways of behaving. This impact can possibly reach out to basic issues like environmentalism, accordingly saddling the force of the medium to advance eco-cognizance.

The Development of Eco-Centered Unscripted television:

Because of developing natural worries, eco-centered unscripted television programs have arisen. These shows, narratives, and docuseries focus on natural issues, preservation endeavors, and economical living practices. They offer watchers a valuable chance to draw in with ecological substance in a configuration they as of now appreciate, making a scaffold among diversion and activism.

Remarkable instances of eco-centered unscripted television incorporate "Planet Earth," "The Blue Planet," and "Long stretches of Living Hazardously." These projects utilize dazzling cinematography and convincing narrating to feature basic natural difficulties, for example, environmental change, deforestation, and untamed life preservation. Thusly, they lift natural issues to a worldwide crowd.

Refining Ecological Activists:

One of the main commitments of eco-centered unscripted television is its capacity to refine natural activists. By exhibiting the individual excursions, difficulties, and commitment of these people, the class scatters generalizations and biases about preservationists. Rather than depicting activists as far off, unique figures, unscripted television presents them as interesting, energetic people who care profoundly about the planet.

Through private stories, watchers can relate to the battles, wins, and inspirations of natural activists, encouraging a more profound association with the reason. This refinement makes a feeling of sympathy and urges watchers to think about their own job in ecological stewardship.

Drawing in a Different Crowd:

Unscripted television has an expansive and different viewership, rising above age, orientation, and financial limits. This range gives a remarkable chance to draw in a wide range of the populace with natural substance. By introducing natural issues in an open and engaging organization, eco-centered unscripted television draws in watchers who probably won't have occupied with natural activism.

This variety of watchers can prompt a more comprehensive and far and wide ecological development. It underlines that ecological issues are not restricted to a specific segment or gathering but rather influence all portions of society. This inclusivity is crucial in tending to the interconnected ecological difficulties we face.

Instructive Worth and Bringing issues to light:

Eco-centered unscripted television fills in as a strong instructive device, conveying complex natural issues in a connecting with and fathomable way. The shocking visuals, convincing accounts, and master critique highlighted in these projects advise watchers about the state regarding the planet, the effect of human exercises, and the dire requirement for activity.

These shows likewise bring issues to light by featuring the magnificence and variety of the regular world. They move stunningness and appreciation for the World's biological systems, encouraging a longing to safeguard and protect them. The close to home association fashioned through eco-centered unscripted television can convert into a feeling of obligation and a pledge to eco-cognizant decisions.

Motivation and Preparation:

Past mindfulness, eco-centered unscripted television has the ability to rouse activity. Watchers are frequently propelled to pursue all the more naturally capable decisions in their regular routines, like lessening energy utilization, supporting protection drives, and embracing economical practices. The individual accounts of activists and their endeavors to make change can act as an impetus for watchers to reach out and have an effect.

Moreover, unscripted television contests like "The Astounding Race" and "Survivor" have coordinated natural difficulties and topics into their episodes. These difficulties underline the significance of collaboration, cleverness, and flexibility with regards to natural manageability, inciting watchers to think about their own capacities to impact change.

Catalyzing Discussions and Support:

Eco-centered unscripted television frequently starts discussions about natural issues, both on the web and disconnected. Watchers participate in conversations, share data, and supporter for change inside their networks. This gradually expanding influence enhances the effect of the programming, making an organization of eco-cognizant people focused on bringing issues to light and driving activity.

Natural associations and activists influence the notoriety of these shows to propel their causes. They cooperate with unscripted television projects to contact a more extensive crowd and team up on preservation projects. This collaboration between media outlets and the natural development broadens the span of promotion endeavors and encourages more noteworthy commitment.

Challenges and Moral Contemplations:

While the convergence of unscripted television and natural activism holds monstrous potential, it isn't without its difficulties and moral contemplations. Pundits contend that sentimentality and amusement worth can in some cases eclipse the reality of natural issues. At times, eco-centered unscripted television may accidentally downplay complex environmental difficulties.

Furthermore, there is a worry that the class can misrepresent ecological arrangements. Tending to environmental change and biodiversity misfortune requires complicated, diverse methodologies, and unscripted television may not necessarily in every case depict the full extent of these difficulties.

One more test is guaranteeing the credibility and respectability of the substance. It is critical that eco-centered unscripted television programs precisely address the science and realities encompassing natural issues and don't overstate or distort them for emotional impact.

The Development of Eco-Centered Unscripted television:

The scene of eco-centered unscripted television keeps on developing. As the criticalness of ecological difficulties develops, so does the interest for content that illuminates and rouses activity. Unscripted television makers and organizations are progressively consolidating eco-cognizant topics into their programming, perceiving the benefit of resolving natural issues.

Streaming stages and online channels have likewise extended the range of eco-centered unscripted television, making it more available to worldwide crowds. This shift towards advanced content takes into account more prominent customization, intelligence, and watcher commitment, further upgrading the effect of natural informing.

The crossing point of unscripted television and ecological activism addresses a strong and compelling collaboration among diversion and backing. Eco-centered unscripted television refines natural activists, connects with a different crowd, instructs watchers, brings issues to light, moves activity, catalyzes discussions, and prepares backing endeavors.

While challenges and moral contemplations exist, the capability of this convergence to drive positive change and encourage a more eco-cognizant society is evident. As ecological issues keep on molding the worldwide plan, unscripted television fills in as an extraordinary stage to enhance the voices of earthy people, share the excellence of the normal world, and move an aggregate obligation to defending the planet for current and people in the future.

Chapter 2

The Contestants

The crossing point of unscripted television and natural activism addresses a dynamic and compelling cooperative energy between two apparently unique universes. Unscripted television, described by its unscripted and frequently sensational substance, has acquired colossal prevalence throughout the course of recent many years. All the while, natural activism has become progressively huge as the world wrestles with earnest biological difficulties. The combination of these two domains has led to a one of a kind stage for raising natural mindfulness, rousing activity, and catalyzing change. In this investigation, we dig into the significant effect and multi-layered nature of the crossing point of unscripted television and ecological activism.

The Prominence and Impact of Unscripted television:

Unscripted television has turned into a worldwide peculiarity, enamoring crowds with a wide cluster of content, from ability contests like "American Symbol" and "The X Element" to docuseries, for example, "The Genuine Housewives" and "Survivor." The class' allure lies in its unscripted, capricious, and engaging nature, which offers watchers a voyeuristic look into the lives, difficulties, and wins of the members.

Unscripted television impacts mainstream society, molding patterns, presenting critical characters, and frequently filling in as a mirror reflecting cultural qualities and ways of behaving. This impact can possibly reach out to basic issues like environmentalism, accordingly bridling the force of the medium to advance eco-cognizance.

The Development of Eco-Centered Unscripted television:

Because of developing natural worries, eco-centered unscripted television programs have arisen. These shows, narratives, and docuseries focus on natural issues, preservation endeavors, and maintainable living practices. They offer watchers a chance to draw in with ecological substance in a configuration they as of now appreciate, making a scaffold among diversion and activism.

Prominent instances of eco-centered unscripted television incorporate "Planet Earth," "The Blue Planet," and "Long stretches of Living Perilously." These projects utilize shocking cinematography and convincing narrating to feature basic natural difficulties, for example, environmental change, deforestation, and untamed life preservation. Thusly, they raise natural issues to a worldwide crowd.

Adapting Ecological Activists:

One of the main commitments of eco-centered unscripted television is its capacity to adapt natural activists. By displaying the individual excursions, difficulties, and commitment of these people, the class disperses generalizations and previously established inclinations about tree huggers. Rather than depicting activists as far off, conceptual figures, unscripted television presents them as interesting, enthusiastic people who care profoundly about the planet.

Through private stories, watchers can relate to the battles, wins, and inspirations of ecological activists, cultivating a more profound association with the reason. This refinement makes a feeling of compassion and urges watchers to think about their own part in ecological stewardship.

Connecting with a Different Crowd:

Unscripted television has a wide and different viewership, rising above age, orientation, and financial limits. This range gives a special chance to draw in a wide range of the populace with natural substance. By introducing natural issues in an open and engaging configuration, eco-centered unscripted television draws in watchers who probably won't have busy with ecological activism.

This variety of watchers can prompt a more comprehensive and far and wide ecological development. It underlines that natural issues are not restricted to a specific segment or gathering but rather influence all fragments of society. This inclusivity is imperative in tending to the interconnected natural difficulties we face.

Instructive Worth and Bringing issues to light:

Eco-centered unscripted television fills in as a strong instructive device, conveying complex natural issues in a connecting with and conceivable way. The dazzling visuals, convincing accounts, and master discourse highlighted in these projects educate watchers about the state regarding the planet, the effect of human exercises, and the dire requirement for activity.

These shows likewise bring issues to light by featuring the excellence and variety of the normal world. They move wonder and appreciation for the World's environments, encouraging a longing to safeguard and save them. The profound association produced through eco-centered unscripted television can convert into a feeling of obligation and a promise to eco-cognizant decisions.

Motivation and Assembly:

Past mindfulness, eco-centered unscripted television has the ability to move activity. Watchers are frequently persuaded to pursue all the more ecologically capable decisions in their day to day routines, like lessening energy utilization, supporting protection drives, and taking on maintainable practices. The individual accounts of activists and their endeavors to make change can act as an impetus for watchers to reach out and have an effect.

Besides, unscripted television rivalries like "The Astounding Race" and "Survivor" have coordinated ecological difficulties and subjects into their episodes. These difficulties accentuate the significance of cooperation, genius, and flexibility with regards to ecological maintainability, inciting watchers to ponder their own capacities to impact change.

Catalyzing Discussions and Promotion:

Eco-centered unscripted television frequently starts discussions about natural issues, both on the web and disconnected. Watchers take part in conversations, share data, and backer for change inside their networks. This gradually expanding influence intensifies the effect of the programming, making an organization of eco-cognizant people focused on bringing issues to light and driving activity.

Ecological associations and activists influence the ubiquity of these shows to propel their causes. They cooperate with unscripted television projects to contact a more extensive crowd and team up on protection projects. This collaboration between media outlets and the ecological development broadens the range of backing endeavors and cultivates more noteworthy commitment.

Challenges and Moral Contemplations:

While the convergence of unscripted television and ecological activism holds enormous potential, it isn't without its difficulties and moral contemplations. Pundits contend that sentimentality and diversion worth can some of the time eclipse the earnestness of ecological issues. Now and again, eco-centered unscripted television may unintentionally downplay complex environmental difficulties.

Moreover, there is a worry that the class can misrepresent natural arrangements. Tending to environmental change and biodiversity misfortune requires mind boggling, multi-layered approaches, and unscripted television may not necessarily depict the full extent of these difficulties.

One more test is guaranteeing the validness and trustworthiness of the substance. It is critical that eco-centered unscripted television programs precisely address the science and realities encompassing natural issues and don't overstate or distort them for emotional impact.

The Development of Eco-Centered Unscripted television:

The scene of eco-centered unscripted television keeps on developing. As the criticalness of ecological difficulties develops, so does the interest for content that illuminates and moves activity. Unscripted television makers and organizations are progressively integrating eco-cognizant topics into their programming, perceiving the benefit of resolving natural issues.

Streaming stages and online channels have likewise extended the range of eco-centered unscripted television, making it more available to worldwide crowds. This shift towards computerized content considers more prominent customization, intelligence, and watcher commitment, further improving the effect of ecological informing.

2.1. Introduction to the eco-warriors

In the domain of unscripted television, the candidates assume a critical part in molding the story, driving the show, and enamoring the crowd. These people, frequently alluded to as "competitors," energetically partake in a wide exhibit of unscripted television shows, going from ability rivalries like "American Symbol" and "The X Variable" to endurance themed projects, for example, "Survivor" and "The Astonishing Race." Every challenger accompanies a novel origin story, range of abilities, and inspiration, making them focal figures in the unscripted television experience. In this investigation, we dive into the multi-layered universe of unscripted television challengers, looking at their inspirations, encounters, and the enduring effect of their support.

Inspirations and Desires:

Candidates truly Programs are propelled by a different scope of elements that drive them to try out and take an interest. These inspirations can be profoundly private and frequently shape the account circular segment of their excursion on the show:

Popularity and Acknowledgment: Numerous competitors look for distinction, acknowledgment, and the chance to send off a lifelong in diversion. They view unscripted television as a stage to grandstand their gifts and gain openness in the business.

Monetary Impetuses: A few competitors are captivated by the possible monetary prizes, including monetary rewards or worthwhile agreements for champs. The commitment of monetary strength can be a strong inspiration.

Individual Test: Others are persuaded by the test and the potential chance to test their abilities, whether in singing, cooking, or getting through in testing conditions. The self-awareness and feeling of achievement are critical prizes.

Energy and Ability: Candidates with a certifiable enthusiasm for their specialty, whether it's singing, cooking, moving, or some other ability, are frequently attracted to unscripted television as a stage to impart their capacities to a more extensive crowd.

Narrating and Support: A few candidates have convincing biographies or causes they are enthusiastic about. They consider unscripted television to be a potential chance to bring issues to light for their story or supporter for a specific issue.

The Projecting System:

The choice of candidates for unscripted television shows includes a thorough projecting cycle. Makers and projecting chiefs survey huge number of tryout tapes, lead meetings, and hold tryouts to pick people who fit explicit standards. These models can differ contingent upon the show's arrangement and goals. Makers intend to make a different and dynamic cast with particular characters and gifts to guarantee a drawing in survey insight.

The projecting system frequently includes surveying a singular's ability as well as their capacity to add to the show's theatrics, clashes, and storyline. This perplexing determination process assumes a critical part in forming the elements and dramatization inside the show.

Difficulties and Battles:

The experience of being an unscripted television contender isn't without its difficulties and battles. Contenders face a scope of hindrances and tensions, both on and off-screen:

Extreme Rivalry: Competitors experience extraordinary contest as they strive for the title, prize, or acknowledgment. The strain to outflank others can prompt pressure, nervousness, and competitions.

Detachment and Bound Day to day environments: In certain shows, candidates are separated from the rest of the world and live in bound conditions. This confinement can be intellectually and genuinely burdening, prompting a scope of responses and difficulties.

Judgment and Analysis: Contenders are dependent upon judgment and analysis from judges, guides, and the crowd. Managing public investigation and pessimistic criticism can sincerely burden.

Loss of Protection: Cooperation truly television frequently implies surrendering a level of security. Candidates are continually observed, and their activities are dependent upon examination, both on and behind the scenes.

Altering and Depiction: how challengers are altered and depicted on the show can affect their public picture. Distortion or being projected in a pessimistic light can lastingly affect their own and proficient lives.

Post-Show Change: Living day to day after unscripted television can be trying for challengers, particularly in the event that they become related with a specific persona or character. Changing back to business as usual or chasing after a profession in their picked field can be an overwhelming cycle.

Winning and Losing:

The results of unscripted television rivalries can differ, for certain hopefuls arising as victors while others experience dissatisfaction. Winning can bring popularity, acknowledgment, and monetary prizes, however it additionally accompanies the strain to satisfy the title and the assumptions that go with it.

Losing, then again, can be a harsh encounter for challengers who put their significant investment into the opposition. Nonetheless, it's fundamental to perceive that not winning doesn't be guaranteed to liken to disappointment. Numerous challengers who didn't win their particular shows have proceeded to make huge progress in their fields.

Challengers as Good examples:

Unscripted television challengers frequently become good examples and wellsprings of motivation for watchers. Their excursions, flexibility, and quest for their fantasies can spur others to pursue their desires and beat difficulties. Contenders who utilize their foundation to advocate for purposes or offer their own battles can turn out to be strong voices for change.

Moreover, portrayal matters in the realm of unscripted television. Challengers from different foundations can act as good examples for people who relate to their encounters, foundations, or personalities, cultivating a feeling of having a place and strengthening.

Influence on Vocations and Individual Lives:

Cooperation truly television can significantly affect challengers' professions and individual lives. A few challengers experience a huge lift in their professions, sending off fruitful ways in media outlets, music, design, or food. For instance, stars like Kelly Clarkson and Jennifer Hudson acquired acclaim through "American Symbol."

Nonetheless, the effect can be positive negative. Hopefuls might battle with the strain of unexpected distinction and the difficulties of keeping a public picture. Dealing with the progress from unscripted television to a feasible profession can be a complex and some of the time slippery undertaking.

Individual lives can likewise be impacted. The consideration and examination that accompany unscripted television distinction can affect challengers' connections, security, and mental prosperity. Competitors might confront the test of offsetting their public personas with their own characters.

Unscripted television as a Stage for Support:

Some unscripted television candidates influence their foundation to advocate for purposes they are enthusiastic about. Whether it's natural protection, civil rights, or psychological well-being mindfulness, contenders have the chance to bring issues to light and activate support for significant issues.

The perceivability and reach of unscripted television can enhance backing endeavors and connect with a more extensive crowd. Hopefuls who utilize their leverage for positive change show the capability of unscripted television as a power for social effect.

Advancement of Unscripted television Hopefuls:

The scene of unscripted television and its contenders keeps on advancing. New shows and organizations arise consistently, offering different open doors for people to feature their abilities, share their accounts, and pursue their fantasies. The projecting system has become more comprehensive, perceiving the significance of different portrayal.

The post-show experience has additionally advanced, with challengers tracking down imaginative ways of benefiting from their distinction. Web-based entertainment and online stages give roads to them to connect straightforwardly with their fan base, market their abilities, and keep up with their presence in the public eye.

2.2. Their diverse backgrounds and motivations

The competitors truly television come from different foundations and carry with them a wide exhibit of inspirations. This variety is a central part of what makes unscripted television so captivating and interesting. Whether it's a singing rivalry, a cooking show, an endurance challenge, or an ability rivalry, the contenders' special stories and inspirations add profundity to the story, resound with watchers, and frequently act as a wellspring of motivation. In this investigation, we dig into the rich embroidery of challengers' experiences and inspirations, featuring how they add to the unique idea of unscripted television.

Various Foundations:

One of the vital qualities of unscripted television is its capacity to exhibit challengers from a large number of foundations. The variety of these foundations frequently mirrors the diverse idea of society, and it permits watchers to interface with hopefuls who come from different backgrounds. These foundations can be comprehensively classified into the accompanying:

Proficient Variety: Hopefuls might have different expert foundations, including educators, specialists, cooks, understudies, business visionaries, or craftsmen. Their callings frequently illuminate their abilities and the interesting abilities they bring to the opposition.

Social and Ethnic Variety: Unscripted television projects frequently reflect social and ethnic variety, praising the extravagance of various legacies and customs. Competitors from different social foundations carry one of a kind points of view and encounters to the show.

Age Variety: Unscripted television isn't restricted to a particular age bunch. Hopefuls length different age sections, from small kids partaking in ability rivalries to grown-ups and seniors taking on many difficulties.

Geological Variety: Competitors hail from various districts, nations, and even mainlands, adding to a worldwide portrayal. The different geological foundations of hopefuls can shape their way to deal with difficulties and assignments on the show.

Financial Variety: Unscripted television grandstands competitors from different financial foundations, from those battling to earn enough to get by to people with critical assets. This variety mirrors the cultural and monetary texture of the crowd.

Instructive Foundations: Candidates might have different instructive levels, including secondary school dropouts, school graduates, and people with postgraduate educations. Their instructive foundations can impact their way to deal with critical thinking and imagination.

Inspirations as Main thrusts:

Competitors are driven by a horde of inspirations that fuel their craving to partake truly television. These inspirations give knowledge into their yearnings, dreams, and individual excursions. The inspirations can be mind boggling and frequently incorporate a mix of elements:

Quest for Notoriety and Acknowledgment: Numerous candidates are attracted to unscripted television by the charm of distinction and the potential chance to earn respect. They see the stage as a take off platform for professions in diversion, whether in music, acting, demonstrating, or other imaginative fields.

Monetary Impetuses: The commitment of monetary prizes, for example, monetary rewards, record arrangements, or support contracts, can be a critical inspiration for competitors. These impetuses offer the chance of monetary solidness and achievement.

Individual Test and Development: A few competitors are inspired by the actual test. They look for self-improvement and are anxious to test their abilities and capacities in a serious climate. Conquering difficulties can be profoundly fulfilling and act as a demonstration of their flexibility and assurance.

Energy for Their Art: Contenders with a veritable enthusiasm for their specialty, whether it's singing, cooking, moving, or some other ability, frequently view unscripted television as a stage to impart their capacities to a more extensive crowd. Their enthusiasm is a main impetus that urges them to participate.

Narrating and Promotion: A few hopefuls have interesting biographies or are enthusiastic supporters for explicit causes. They use unscripted television as a way to share their encounters, bring issues to light for issues they care about, or advocate for change. Their inspirations reach out past private increase to more extensive social effect.

Craving for Individual Change: For certain candidates, unscripted television addresses a chance for individual change. They might be hoping to break out of their usual ranges of familiarity, challenge themselves, or rehash their lives. The groundbreaking capability of the experience is their essential inspiration.

Individual Stories and Histories:

Competitors frequently accompany convincing individual stories and histories that add profundity to their characters on unscripted television. These accounts are much of the time featured throughout the show, making profound associations with the crowd. A few normal kinds of individual stories and histories include:

Beating Misfortune: Contenders who have conquered critical difficulties, like disease, individual misfortune, or financial difficulty, frequently share their accounts as a wellspring of motivation. These people can act as reference points of strength and expectation for watchers confronting comparative challenges.

Seeking after Unfulfilled Dreams: A few candidates join unscripted television to pursue dreams they have long held onto however not yet had the valuable chance to seek after. Whether it's an energy for singing, cooking, or experience, unscripted television gives a stage to understand these yearnings.

Family and Social Foundation: Competitors from different social foundations might share stories connected with their family legacy, customs, and the assumptions for their networks. These accounts can give social bits of knowledge and feature the intricacies of personality.

Groundbreaking Encounters: Individual stories frequently include extraordinary encounters, like travel, charitable effort, or individual changes. Challengers who have had encounters that have significantly impacted them can offer interesting viewpoints and experiences.

Local area Commitment and Activism: A few candidates utilize their experience on unscripted television to exhibit their contribution in local area commitment, activism, or magnanimity. These accounts act as a way to bring issues to light for significant causes.

Projecting and Choice Interaction:

The projecting system for unscripted television shows is a basic part in the choice of contenders. Makers and projecting chiefs are entrusted with recognizing people who fit explicit models as well as have convincing stories and inspirations. The projecting system normally includes the accompanying advances:

Tryout Tapes: Contenders submit tryout tapes, giving a brief look at their characters, gifts, and inspirations. These tapes act as the underlying evaluating instrument for projecting chiefs.

Meetings and Tryouts: Shortlisted applicants are welcome to take part in meetings and tryouts. These in-person connections permit projecting chiefs to survey the challengers' reasonableness for the show and their similarity with the cast.

Variety Contemplations: Projecting chiefs endeavor to make different projects that mirror a large number of foundations, ages, and encounters. The objective is to offer a far reaching portrayal of society.

Story Curves and Struggle Elements: Makers frequently evaluate how hopefuls' inspirations and stories can add to the account bend and struggle elements of the show. They look for people who will bring show, kinship, and profound profundity to the program.

Character Improvement: Competitors are not simply chosen in light of their experiences and inspirations; they are additionally picked for their true capacity as characters inside the show. Makers might choose contenders with differentiating characters and inspirations to make convincing on-screen communications.

Effect of Variety and Inspirations:

The presence of candidates from assorted foundations and with shifted inspirations altogether advances the unscripted television experience. This variety:

Draws in a More extensive Crowd: A different cast can connect with a greater and fluctuated crowd. Watchers from various foundations can associate with hopefuls who share their social, expert, or individual encounters.

Mirrors the Intricacy of Society: Unscripted television can act as a mirror to society, mirroring its complex nature. The consideration of challengers with assorted foundations reflects the variety present in reality.

Cultivates Sympathy and Understanding: Competitors' inspirations and origin stories frequently lead to a feeling of compassion and understanding among watchers. This compassion can stretch out to people and gatherings who might have been already new to the watcher.

Moves and Empowers: Contenders' inspirations, particularly when attached to individual accounts of conquering difficulty or chasing after dreams, can motivate and urge watchers to seek after their own goals and face their difficulties.

Drives Interest and Commitment: The variety of inspirations, combined with the differentiation of foundations and characters, frequently drives interest and commitment to the show. Watchers become put resources into the candidates' excursions, adding to the show's allure.

2.3. The selection process

The choice cycle for unscripted television shows is a complex and diverse method that assumes a critical part in molding the piece of the cast and, thusly, the general progress of the program. Projecting chiefs and makers are answerable for distinguishing people who fit the show's particular models as well as can possibly add to drawing in accounts, clashes, and dramatization. This interaction is set apart by a progression of steps that take into consideration the cautious assessment of competitors and their reasonableness for the show. In this investigation, we dig into the complexities of the choice cycle, revealing insight into the means, contemplations, and the effect of this basic part of unscripted television creation.

Projecting Goals and Rules:

Before the choice interaction starts, it is fundamental for the creation group to lay out the goals and measures for projecting. These targets might shift relying upon the show's arrangement and objectives however ordinarily incorporate the accompanying contemplations:

Variety: Makers expect to make projects that are assorted concerning age, orientation, foundation, nationality, and characters. Variety reflects society as well as adds to the intricacy of on-screen communications.

Ability and Abilities: The show's particular arrangement decides the abilities and gifts expected of contenders. For instance, a cooking rivalry might look for challengers with culinary mastery, while an ability show might require a different scope of creative capacities.

Character and Similarity: Hopefuls' characters assume a huge part in the determination cycle. Makers search for people with differentiating characters to make dynamic associations, clashes, and brotherhood.

Inspiration and Narrating: Hopefuls' inspirations, individual stories, and desires are thought of, as these elements add to connecting with account bends. Makers might look for contenders with exceptional and convincing inspirations that can reverberate with the crowd.

Struggle Elements: Makers evaluate how competitors' characters and inspirations might make struggle or dramatization inside the show. These contentions are fundamental for producing watcher interest and commitment.

Tryout Tapes and Entries:

The underlying move toward the choice cycle normally includes contenders submitting tryout tapes or applications. These tryout tapes act as competitors' most memorable chance to establish an ideal connection with projecting chiefs and makers. The substance of these tapes might include:

Presentation: Candidates present themselves, giving their name, age, and a concise outline of their experience.

Gifts and Abilities: On the off chance that the show is ability centered, contenders exhibit their capacities, like singing, moving, cooking, or different abilities applicable to the show's configuration.

Inspiration: Competitors frequently talk about their inspirations for partaking in the show. They might make sense of their energy for their specialty, their goals, or their own accounts.

Character: Competitors are urged to allow their characters to sparkle in their tryout tapes. Projecting chiefs search for people who are drawing in, dynamic, and appealing.

History: A few competitors might share individual stories or difficulties they have survived, as these accounts can be sincerely convincing and reverberate with the crowd.

Meetings and Tryouts:

Shortlisted up-and-comers are regularly welcomed to take part in interviews and in-person tries out. These meetings and tryouts offer projecting chiefs and makers the chance to evaluate the competitors more meticulously. Key components of the meeting and tryout process include:

Evaluation of Character: Meetings permit projecting chiefs to survey the competitors' characters, relational abilities, and capacity to draw in with the creation group. Character elements are urgent to the progress of the show.

Displaying Abilities and Abilities: In-person tries out furnish challengers with the opportunity to feature their gifts and abilities to a greater extent. This step permits makers to assess the competitors' capacities firsthand.

Similarity and Struggle Potential: Projecting chiefs consider the similarity of expected candidates and how their characters could connect inside the show. Makers look for a blend of characters that can prompt intriguing struggles, unions, and fellowship.

Narrating and Inspiration: During interviews, challengers have the chance to expound on their inspirations and individual stories. Projecting chiefs survey how these inspirations can add to connecting with story bends.

Mental Assessment and Historical verifications:

Now and again, contenders go through mental assessments as a feature of the determination cycle. These assessments are pointed toward recognizing people who might experience issues adapting to the close to home and mental requests of unscripted television. The prosperity of the hopefuls is fundamentally important, and makers mean to guarantee that they can deal with the tensions and difficulties of the show.

Furthermore, record verifications are commonly led to confirm challengers' personalities and foundations. These checks assist with guaranteeing the credibility and trustworthiness of the choice cycle.

Thought of Crowd Allure:

Makers think about the expected allure of contenders to the show's main interest group. They intend to choose people who will resound with watchers and make profound associations. Hopefuls who have appealing foundations, inspirations, or characters are frequently favored on the grounds that they can upgrade the watcher's commitment with the program.

Projecting for Story Curves:

The story bend of the show is a critical thought during the choice cycle. Makers look for people who can add to convincing storylines, clashes, and show. Contenders with novel inspirations, goals, and individual stories are in many cases picked in light of the fact that these components add profundity and intricacy to the show.

Projecting chiefs additionally evaluate how competitors might associate with each other and whether their connections can drive the story forward. Similarity and clashes are painstakingly thought of, as they can prompt connecting on-screen elements.

Choice for Science and Attachment:

The science between candidates is a significant calculate the determination interaction. Makers mean to make projects in which the characters and inspirations of competitors supplement and difference with each other. Union inside the gathering is likewise really important, as it adds to the general elements of the show.

Lawful and Legally binding Arrangements:

Whenever candidates are chosen, they commonly go through legitimate and legally binding arrangements. These arrangements frame the agreements of cooperation, including rules, assumptions, and any expected remuneration or prizes. Candidates should know about the authoritative commitments and lawful parts of their investment.

Variety and Inclusivity:

Lately, there has been an expanded accentuation on variety and inclusivity in actuality television projecting. Makers are aware of the significance of addressing an expansive scope of foundations, personalities, and viewpoints. The determination interaction is intended to guarantee that projects are comprehensive and mirror the variety of society.

Variety contemplations likewise reach out to mature, orientation, sexual direction, and capacities. Unscripted television tries to celebrate and feature contenders from varying backgrounds.

Effect of the Choice Cycle:

The choice cycle is a basic part in the progress of unscripted television shows. The cautious assessment of candidates, their inspirations, and their similarity with each other assumes a significant part in molding the show's elements and story. The effect of the determination cycle reaches out to:

Commitment and Watcher Association: A very much chose cast draws in the crowd and cultivates an association among watchers and competitors. Appealing inspirations, individual stories, and different foundations improve watcher commitment.

Story Improvement: The choice of competitors with exceptional inspirations, goals, and characters adds to convincing account circular segments. Makers intend to make storylines that catch the crowd's consideration.

Struggle and Show: The choice interaction tries to recognize competitors who can create clashes, unions, and dramatization inside the show. These elements are fundamental for supporting watcher interest.

Portrayal and Inclusivity: Projecting chiefs and makers are aware of the requirement for portrayal and inclusivity. The choice cycle adds to the more extensive objective of mirroring society's variety.

Watcher Sympathy and Motivation: Candidates' inspirations and individual stories frequently lead to watcher compassion and motivation. Watchers are attracted to competitors who face difficulties, seek after their fantasies, or promoter for purposes.

Chapter 3

Eco-Challenges

As we venture further into the 21st hundred years, we end up defied with a variety of considerable eco-challenges. These difficulties, molded by human exercises, represent a danger to the fragile balance of our planet's biological systems. In a world set apart by a rising worldwide populace, quick industrialization, and a consistently extending interest for normal assets, the tension on the climate has arrived at uncommon levels. In this exposition, we will investigate the absolute most squeezing eco-difficulties within recent memory, analyzing their causes, outcomes, and likely arrangements.

One of the most noticeable eco-challenges we face is environmental change. The World's environment is changing at a disturbing rate, essentially because of the emanation of ozone harming substances, like carbon dioxide and methane, into the climate. These gases trap heat, prompting a steady expansion in worldwide temperatures, a peculiarity known as an unnatural weather change. The results of environmental change are now clear, with rising ocean levels, more regular and extreme climate occasions, and changes in biological systems. The effect on biodiversity is huge, as species battle to adjust to changing circumstances or face termination.

Deforestation is another major eco-challenge. The world's backwoods, frequently alluded to as the "lungs of the Earth," are overall quickly drained to clear a path for horticulture, metropolitan turn of events, and the creation of wood and paper items. Deforestation not just decreases the World's ability to assimilate carbon dioxide yet additionally brings about the deficiency of critical natural surroundings for innumerable species. It disturbs the equilibrium of environments and adds to environmental change.

At the same time, the debasement of our seas and marine environments presents a significant eco-challenge. Overfishing, contamination, and the obliteration of beach front environments have negatively affected the soundness of our seas. Coral reefs, for instance, are experiencing dying occasions brought about by warming waters and expanded acridity, prompting the deficiency of biodiversity and adversely affecting the jobs of seaside networks that depend on fisheries.

The exhaustion of freshwater assets is another basic eco-challenge. As the world-wide populace keeps on developing, the interest for spotless and available freshwater increments. Nonetheless, contamination, wasteful water use, and the adjustment of stream courses have prompted water shortage in numerous districts. This shortage influences drinking water supplies as well as has sweeping ramifications for horticulture and industry.

The deficiency of biodiversity is a worldwide eco-challenge that remains inseparable with a considerable lot of different difficulties we face. As environments are obliterated, species are driven to the edge of eradication. Biodiversity isn't simply a question of safeguarding charming creatures; it is crucial for the solidness of environments and the administrations they give, for example, fertilization, infectious prevention, and carbon sequestration. The deficiency of biodiversity has significant ramifications for human prosperity.

Contamination, in its different structures, is an unavoidable eco-challenge. Air contamination from modern discharges and transportation influences human well-being as well as harms biological systems. Water contamination from rural overflow, modern releases, and inappropriate garbage removal taints streams, lakes, and seas, compromising oceanic life and human admittance to clean water. Soil contamination debases agrarian grounds and decreases their efficiency.

The abuse of pesticides and compound manures in horticulture is an eco-challenge with serious results. While these synthetic compounds have supported crop yields, they have likewise hurt the climate. Pesticides kill bothers as well as valuable bugs, birds, and different creatures. Additionally, synthetic composts can filter into water bodies, causing water contamination and hurting amphibian life.

The fast urbanization and extension of urban areas address a special arrangement of eco-challenges. As additional individuals move to metropolitan regions, the interest for lodging, foundation, and energy increments. Never-ending suburbia consumes significant agrarian land and normal living spaces, adding to territory misfortune and biodiversity decline. Besides, the amassed energy utilization in urban areas brings about raised discharges of ozone harming substances and air contamination.

The creation and removal of plastics have arisen as a significant eco-challenge. Plastics are adaptable and strong materials, yet their tirelessness in the climate presents critical issues. Plastic waste collects in landfills, seas, and streams, hurting natural life and filtering poisonous synthetics into the climate. Microplastics, minuscule particles that outcome from the breakdown of bigger plastic things, have penetrated even the most remote corners of the Earth, raising worries about their effect on environments and human wellbeing.

Land corruption, frequently brought about by impractical farming practices and deforestation, is a huge eco-challenge. Soil disintegration, loss of dirt, and desertification can deliver once-ripe grounds inefficient. This prompts food instability, dislodging of networks, and expanded tension on normal assets.

The deficiency of wetlands is another eco-challenge that has broad results. Wetlands, like bogs, swamps, and marshes, assume fundamental parts in managing water stream, separating poisons, and giving territory to assorted species. Their annihilation disturbs these imperative capabilities and adds to flooding, water contamination, and biodiversity misfortune.

The abuse and abuse of anti-toxins in human and creature wellbeing present an eco-challenge with concerning suggestions. The rise of anti-microbial safe microorganisms, or superbugs, undermines general wellbeing and farming practices. It imperils our capacity to treat irresistible illnesses really, and the spread of anti-infection deposits in the climate adds to the issue.

The fast decrease in bumble bee populaces is a squeezing eco-challenge, as these bugs are vital for pollinating large numbers of the world's harvests. Settlement breakdown jumble, natural surroundings misfortune, pesticide openness, and sickness play all played parts in the decay of bumble bee populaces. The outcomes incorporate diminished crop yields and potential food security issues.

Metropolitan intensity islands are a developing eco-challenge related with environmental change and urbanization. As urban areas grow, they ingest and hold heat, prompting higher temperatures inside metropolitan regions. This compounds the impacts of heatwaves, increments energy utilization for cooling, and adversely influences human wellbeing.

Another eco-challenge is the exhaustion of ozone in the World's stratosphere. While global endeavors have effectively decreased the creation and utilization of ozone-draining substances, the recuperation of the ozone layer stays a drawn out process. The diminishing of the ozone layer opens us to destructive bright radiation, which can cause skin malignant growth, waterfalls, and other medical conditions.

Intrusive species are a developing eco-challenge, frequently worked with by world-wide exchange and travel. These non-local species can disturb environments by out-competing local species, spreading illnesses, and adjusting the design and capability of normal networks.

The change to sustainable power sources is both an answer for eco-challenges and a test in itself. While the shift away from petroleum products can diminish ozone harming substance emanations and battle environmental change, it likewise presents difficulties connected with energy capacity, framework, and the financial effects on locales intensely reliant upon the non-renewable energy source industry.

The issue of waste administration is an unavoidable eco-challenge, particularly in thickly populated metropolitan regions. The ill-advised removal of waste, including electronic waste (e-squander), brings about natural tainting and wellbeing risks for those living in nearness to landfills and dumpsites.

The deficiency of dirt is an eco-challenge that undermines agrarian efficiency and food security. Dirt, the highest layer of soil, is wealthy in supplements and fundamental for plant development. Impractical horticultural practices, deforestation, and disintegration are exhausting this important asset.

The eco-challenge of territory fracture emerges from human exercises, for example, metropolitan turn of events and street development, what partition regular scenes into more modest, secluded patches. This can upset the development of natural life, disturb environments, and lead to hereditary disconnection among populaces.

3.1. Description of the eco-challenge format

In tending to the diverse and squeezing eco-difficulties of the 21st 100 years, it is essential to lay out a far reaching design that considers a careful comprehension of each issue. The eco-challenge design introduced here is expected to offer an incorporating structure for the assessment of different natural issues, their causes, outcomes, and possible arrangements. This configuration fills in as an aide for diving into the intricacies of each eco-challenge, cultivating informed conversations, and driving aggregate activity towards reasonable arrangements.

Presentation: Outlining the Eco-Challenge

Setting the Stage: The presentation makes way for the conversation of a specific eco-challenge, offering setting and foundation data. It portrays the meaning of the issue in the bigger setting of worldwide ecological worries.

Distinguishing proof of the Test: Obviously recognizing the eco-challenge is principal. This incorporates portraying its key parts, like the main impetuses, scope, and the impacted environments, species, or networks.

Significance: Featuring the pertinence of the eco-challenge to human culture and the climate is fundamental. This segment frames why the issue matters and who is influenced by it, accentuating the interconnections between natural difficulties and human prosperity.

Causes and Drivers: Unloading the Basic Elements

Human Exercises: An eco-challenge frequently emerges from human exercises, like industrialization, urbanization, deforestation, or contamination. This part digs into the particular human activities that add to the test.

Regular Factors: Some eco-difficulties might have normal parts, like environment changeability or topographical occasions. Here, the job of regular variables in the test is investigated.

Interconnected Causes: Generally speaking, different variables, both human-instigated and regular, associate to make or intensify eco-challenges. Understanding these intricate interconnections is basic to tracking down compelling arrangements.

Results: Disclosing the Effects and Consequences

Natural Effects: This part explains the immediate and aberrant outcomes of the eco-challenge on the climate. It talks about changes in environments, biodiversity misfortune, changes in environment designs, and other appropriate biological impacts.

Financial Effects: The results of eco-challenges stretch out past the regular world to influence human social orders. This remembers influences for jobs, wellbeing, food security, and monetary strength.

Flowing Impacts: Frequently, an eco-challenge's ramifications can set off a chain response of different issues. This segment investigates how the test swells through interconnected frameworks, prompting further issues.

Current Endeavors and Drives: What Has Been Finished?

Strategy Measures: Numerous state run administrations and global associations have done whatever it takes to address eco-challenges. This part looks at existing approaches, guidelines, and arrangements pointed toward alleviating or settling the issue.

Examination and Advancement: Researchers, scientists, and trend-setters are effectively taken part in understanding and tending to eco-challenges. This part features continuous exploration and mechanical developments that proposition guarantee in fighting the issue.

Local area and Grassroots Activity: Neighborhood people group, non-legislative associations (NGOs), and grassroots developments frequently assume a critical part in tending to eco-challenges. This segment underlines the endeavors made at local area and individual levels.

Difficulties and Detours: Snags to Advance

Political and Monetary Obstacles: Political and financial interests can at times ruin progress in tending to eco-challenges. This segment investigates the difficulties connected with strategy execution and monetary powers that oppose change.

Mechanical and Information Holes: Advances in innovation and logical comprehension are critical for tending to eco-challenges. Recognizing holes in information and innovation gives knowledge into where further exploration or development is required.

Conduct and Social Elements: Changing human way of behaving and social standards can challenge. This segment tends to the sociocultural elements that obstruct progress in handling eco-challenges.

Future Possibilities: What Lies Ahead?

Expecting Change: This part offers a point of view on how the eco-challenge is probably going to develop from now on, taking into account factors like populace development, urbanization, and arising innovations.

Situations and Projections: Investigating conceivable future situations and projections for the eco-challenge helps in evaluating its seriousness and the desperation of activity.

Mechanical and Strategy Advancements: Developments and strategy changes that could hold guarantee in tending to the eco-challenge are examined in this part.

Arrangements and Procedures: Exploring the Way ahead

Alleviation Techniques: The essential spotlight here is on measures that can lessen the effects and seriousness of the eco-challenge. This might incorporate approaches, innovations, and conduct changes.

Variation Measures: For some eco-challenges, transformation is important to adapt to continuous or inescapable changes. Methodologies for adjusting to the new real factors brought about by the eco-challenge are investigated.

Anticipation and Readiness: now and again, the best methodology is to keep the test from deteriorating or plan for its likely outcomes. This segment inspects proactive measures that can be taken.

Worldwide Viewpoint: The Interconnected Idea of Eco-Difficulties

Worldwide Joint efforts: Numerous eco-challenges rise above public boundaries. This segment features the significance of worldwide participation and arrangements in resolving these worldwide issues.

Overflow Impacts: The interconnectedness of eco-challenges implies that advancement in resolving one issue can have overflow consequences for other people. Inspecting these communications is vital for an all encompassing way to deal with ecological difficulties.

Feasible Improvement Objectives (SDGs): The eco-challenge arrangement can be connected to the Assembled Countries' SDGs, representing how tending to eco-challenges lines up with the more extensive worldwide objectives for manageability.

Determination: A Source of inspiration

Outline of Central issues: The end concisely sums up the principal discoveries and bits of knowledge from the eco-challenge conversation.

Accentuation on Earnestness: Finishing up with an accentuation on the direness of tending to the eco-challenge empowers activity and highlights the significance of aggregate liability.

Strengthening and Activation: The end additionally features the job of people, networks, associations, and states in tending to the eco-challenge and the force of aggregate activity.

References: Refering to Sources

Insightful Sources: This part records the academic articles, reports, and books referred to all through the conversation, giving validity and amazing chances to additional perusing and examination.

The eco-challenge design introduced here gives an organized way to deal with understanding and resolving the basic natural issues within recent memory. By methodicallly inspecting the causes, results, existing endeavors, difficulties, and likely arrangements, we can encourage a more profound comprehension of these eco-difficulties and work together to track down feasible and successful ways of moderating and resolve them. This configuration fills in as a device for informed discourse, direction, and the quest for a more supportable and amicable relationship with our planet.

3.2. Examples of specific challenges

In the huge scene of eco-challenges, it is fundamental to investigate explicit guides to acquire a more significant comprehension of this present reality issues we face. These models represent the intricacies, results, and potential arrangements related with different ecological issues. Here, we dive into a few critical eco-challenges that range the range of natural issues, from environmental change and biodiversity misfortune to contamination and asset exhaustion.

Environmental Change: The Test of Our Time

Environmental change is seemingly the most squeezing and including eco-challenge within recent memory. It results fundamentally from the collection of ozone harming substances in the World's environment, basically carbon dioxide (CO2) and methane (CH4). These gases trap intensity and lead to climbing worldwide temperatures, a peculiarity known as an unnatural weather change. The results of environmental change are complex and inescapable.

One explicit illustration of the test presented by environmental change is the sped up liquefying of polar ice covers. In the Cold, the fast retreat of ocean ice has broad impacts, remembering rising ocean levels and changes for sea course designs. These progressions disturb environments and have suggestions for worldwide environment frameworks.

Furthermore, outrageous climate occasions, like tropical storms, heatwaves, and dry seasons, are increasing because of environmental change. These occasions lead to expanded financial misfortunes, dislodging of networks, and dangers to food security. Weak populaces, especially in low-lying beach front regions, are lopsidedly impacted.

Relieving environmental change includes a mind boggling trap of systems, including progressing to environmentally friendly power sources, upgrading energy proficiency, and advancing supportable land use rehearses. Peaceful accords like the Paris Understanding plan to unite nations to control ozone depleting substance outflows and breaking point an Earth-wide temperature boost.

Deforestation: The Lungs of the Earth Under Danger

Deforestation is a pivotal eco-challenge driven by human exercises, fundamentally to clear a path for farming, metropolitan development, and the creation of wood and paper items. This prompts the deficiency of indispensable woodland biological systems and has critical ecological outcomes.

The Amazon rainforest, frequently alluded to as the "lungs of the Earth," is a great representation of deforestation's worldwide effect. Broad getting free from the Amazon for farming, logging, and foundation improvement brings about the deficiency of biodiversity as well as adds to environmental change. Woodlands are carbon sinks, engrossing carbon dioxide from the environment. The deficiency of woodlands, similar to the Amazon, expands the grouping of CO2 in the environment, fueling a worldwide temperature alteration.

The deforestation challenge includes tracking down reasonable choices to satisfy the world's developing need for assets while protecting fundamental woodland biological systems. Drives like reforestation and afforestation, as well as dependable ranger service rehearses, expect to work out some kind of harmony between asset use and preservation.

Sea Debasement: A Quiet Emergency Submerged

The world's seas are indispensable for life on The planet, yet they face a bunch of eco-challenges, including overfishing, contamination, and natural surroundings obliteration. Coral reefs, perhaps of the most different and useful marine environment, are a strong illustration of this test.

Coral reefs are experiencing mass dying occasions, principally because of warming ocean temperatures and expanded sea sharpness, both connected to environmental change. The deficiency of coral reefs has obliterating ramifications for marine biodiversity and the vocations of millions of individuals who rely upon them for food and pay.

Overfishing is one more aspect of the sea debasement challenge. Impractical fishing rehearses exhaust fish populaces, upset marine food networks, and compromise the drawn out maintainability of fisheries. This challenge requires the execution of better fisheries the executives, including guidelines, portions, and marine safeguarded regions.

Battling sea contamination, brought about by plastic waste, oil slicks, and modern releases, is one more basic part of this eco-challenge. Advancements in squander the executives, including diminishing single-use plastics and creating advancements for plastic cleanup, are fundamental for resolving this issue.

Freshwater Shortage: The Decreasing Asset

Admittance to freshwater is basic to human existence, yet freshwater shortage is a developing eco-challenge. The Aral Ocean, when one of the world's biggest inland waterways, fills in as a piercing illustration of the results of blundered water assets.

Unnecessary water system for farming, combined with the redirection of streams for different purposes, made the Aral Ocean contract decisively. The ocean's drying up has had serious financial and natural repercussions, including the interruption of fishing businesses and the arrival of harmful residue from the uncovered lakebed.

In many regions of the planet, freshwater shortage prompts rivalry for restricted assets, and it could add to struggle. Maintainable water the board rehearses, for example, productive water system, water gathering, and the insurance of wetlands, are fundamental for tending to this eco-challenge.

Biodiversity Misfortune: The Unwinding Web of Life

Biodiversity misfortune, driven by living space obliteration, intrusive species, contamination, and overexploitation, is an unavoidable eco-challenge with worldwide results. The deficiency of biodiversity isn't just about the termination of alluring species; it compromises the solidness and versatility of biological systems.

One illustration of biodiversity misfortune is the decay of the ruler butterfly populace. The obliteration of milkweed living spaces, where ruler butterflies lay their eggs and their hatchlings feed, has brought about a huge diminishing in their numbers. This decline has flowing impacts, influencing different species that depend on rulers as a food source and pollinators.

Preservation endeavors to address biodiversity misfortune incorporate the foundation of safeguarded regions, environment reclamation, and measures to diminish the presentation of obtrusive species. Additionally, maintainable practices in horticulture, ranger service, and fisheries can assist with safeguarding biodiversity.

Contamination: Foreign substances in Our Current circumstance

Contamination is a diverse eco-challenge that incorporates different structures, including air contamination, water contamination, and soil tainting. The contamination of waterways and lakes, similar to the instance of the Chesapeake Narrows in the US, outlines the significant environmental results of contamination.

Abundance supplements from agrarian spillover and sewage release into the Chesapeake Cove have prompted water quality issues, including algal blossoms and oxygen-exhausted "no man's lands." These issues hurt sea-going life, disturb fisheries, and undermine the vocations of beach front networks.

Contamination control measures include stricter natural guidelines, contamination checking, and the reception of cleaner advancements. Public mindfulness missions and local area drives assume a part in decreasing contamination at the individual and nearby levels.

Farming Difficulties: Pesticides and Soil Corruption

Farming is a foundation of human development, however it likewise presents huge eco-challenges. The abuse of pesticides, for example, neonicotinoids, embodies the biological outcomes of specific cultivating rehearses.

Neonicotinoids, a class of insect poisons, have been connected to the downfall of pollinators, including bumble bees. These synthetic compounds upset the sensory systems of honey bees, influencing their searching and route capacities. This, thusly, influences crop fertilization and food creation.

Soil debasement is another rural eco-challenge. Impractical practices, similar to monoculture and over the top utilization of synthetic manures, drain dirt and lessen its fruitfulness. Soil disintegration, as exemplified by the Residue Bowl in the US during the 1930s, can bring about the deficiency of arable land and food frailty.

Supportable rural practices, like natural cultivating, incorporated bother the board, and soil protection strategies, offer answers for alleviate these difficulties.

Urbanization: The Extending Impression of Urban areas

The quick development of urban areas and metropolitan regions presents remarkable ecological difficulties. Urbanization prompts the extension of constructed conditions to the detriment of normal scenes, a peculiarity known as endless suburbia.

Metropolitan intensity islands, which are restricted areas of raised temperatures in urban communities, are a consequence of urbanization. These regions experience higher temperatures because of the ingestion and maintenance of intensity by cement and black-top. Metropolitan intensity islands intensify the impacts of heatwaves and increment energy utilization for cooling.

Feasible metropolitan preparation and plan, as well as the improvement of green framework, offer answers for alleviate the difficulties of urbanization. These techniques intend to make more reasonable and harmless to the ecosystem urban communities.

Plastic Contamination: The Determined Hazard

The creation and removal of plastics have arisen as a significant eco-challenge. Plastics are strong and flexible materials, however their constancy in the climate represents a critical issue. Microplastics, minuscule particles coming about because of the breakdown of bigger plastic things, represent this test.

Microplastics have penetrated even the most distant region of the planet, including the profound sea and Cold ice. These particles not just mischief marine life that ingests or collaborates with them yet additionally raise worries about their possible effect on human wellbeing through the order of things.

Tending to plastic contamination includes decreasing plastic use, advancing reusing and legitimate garbage removal, and creating imaginative strategies for plastic cleanup and reusing.

3.3. The importance of eco-education within challenges

Despite steadily mounting natural difficulties, eco-training arises as a urgent mainstay of our aggregate endeavors to relieve, adjust to, and eventually defeat these major problems. Eco-instruction, incorporating natural schooling and environmental education, outfits people and social orders with the information, abilities, and values important to comprehend, appreciate, and address eco-challenges actually. In this complete conversation, we dig into the significant meaning of eco-training inside the setting of the complex natural difficulties we defy in the 21st hundred years.

Figuring out Eco-Schooling

Eco-training, comprehensively characterized, includes the instructive techniques and drives pointed toward upgrading's comprehension people might interpret the climate, the complicated trap of natural frameworks, and the difficulties that compromise these frameworks. It isn't restricted to customary homeroom settings however stretches out to a different exhibit of casual and non-formal instructive open doors, including local area programs, nature focuses, online stages, and public mindfulness crusades.

Eco-Training and Mindfulness: The Groundwork of Natural Stewardship

Eco-schooling establishes the groundwork for natural mindfulness, developing a feeling of obligation towards the regular world. It ingrains a comprehension of the natural worth of biological systems, species, and the administrations they give. By supporting natural mindfulness, eco-instruction encourages a profound association with the climate, moving people to turn out to be better stewards of the planet.

Consider environmental change, one of the most imposing eco-challenges. Eco-schooling is instrumental in conveying the logical agreement on environmental change, the job of human exercises, and the results of a dangerous atmospheric devation. This information enables people to settle on informed decisions, lessen their carbon impression, and supporter for arrangements that relieve environmental change.

Eco-Schooling and Biodiversity Preservation

Biodiversity misfortune, driven by living space obliteration, obtrusive species, and contamination, is an unavoidable eco-challenge. Eco-training is major in advancing biodiversity protection. It gives bits of knowledge into the interconnectedness of biological systems and the job of every species inside them. By featuring the significance of biodiversity, eco-instruction energizes the assurance and reclamation of basic living spaces and the mindful administration of normal assets.

In this specific situation, drives like the Ruler butterfly preservation programs, which teach general society about the significance of pollinators and their compromised status, epitomize the force of eco-training. These projects bring issues to light and connect with networks in establishing local milkweed to help the Ruler butterfly populace.

Eco-Training and Reasonable Asset The executives

Freshwater shortage and asset exhaustion are huge eco-challenges. Eco-instruction outfits people with the information and abilities to reasonably oversee assets. It underlines the standards of water preservation, dependable energy use, and decreasing waste. By encouraging a culture of asset effectiveness, eco-training adds to tending to these difficulties at the individual and local area levels.

The progress to practical horticulture is another region where eco-schooling assumes a significant part. Drives like permaculture configuration courses grant information about regenerative cultivating works on, including crop pivot, fertilizing the soil, and natural planting. By teaching people about practical agribusiness, eco-schooling advances versatility despite horticultural eco-challenges like soil debasement and pesticide abuse.

Eco-Schooling and Contamination Alleviation

Contamination, in its different structures, is an unavoidable eco-challenge. Eco-schooling fills in as an incredible asset in tending to contamination. It instructs people about the sources and results of contamination, empowering capable utilization and waste decrease. This, thusly, decreases the contamination load on biological systems and limits the effect on human wellbeing.

Think about plastic contamination, a noticeable and tenacious test. Eco-training efforts spotlight the adverse impacts of single-use plastics and illuminate general society about the significance regarding lessening plastic waste. These missions rouse social changes, for example, the decrease of plastic use and support in ocean side cleanups and waste reusing programs.

Eco-Schooling and Environmental Change Moderation

The issue of environmental change, coming from the outflow of ozone harming substances, is maybe the most basic eco-challenge of our period. Eco-training assumes a focal part in environmental change moderation by bringing issues to light about the science, causes, and outcomes of an Earth-wide temperature boost. It additionally advances social changes that diminish fossil fuel byproducts and support reasonable living practices.

Environment proficiency is a fundamental part of eco-training. Grasping the rudiments of environment science, ozone depleting substance emanations, and environment models is fundamental for informed navigation. Eco-training attempts, from school educational programs to online assets, assist people with embracing these principal ideas.

Eco-Training and Reasonable Ways of life

Eco-schooling impacts customer conduct and supports the reception of manageable ways of life. By illuminating people about the natural effects regarding their decisions, it engages them to go with eco-cognizant choices in regards to transportation, energy use, diet, and item utilization.

The eco-challenge of urbanization, described by the development of urban communities and the ascent of metropolitan intensity islands, gives an unmistakable illustration of the job of eco-schooling in encouraging reasonable metropolitan living. Eco-schooling efforts in metropolitan regions frequently advocate for energy-proficient structures, public transportation, green spaces, and roof gardens. These drives motivate occupants to partake in economical metropolitan preparation and advancement.

Eco-Training for Inclusivity and Value

Eco-training reaches out past information spread; it includes the standards of inclusivity and value. Tending to eco-challenges requires perceiving and tending to the abberations in natural effects. Weak people group frequently endure the worst part of natural issues, for example, contamination and environmental change, because of financial elements.

Eco-training plans to connect these differences by making natural information available to all, paying little heed to mature, orientation, financial status, or social foundation. It stresses the significance of natural equity and urges underestimated networks to participate in dynamic cycles connected with eco-challenges.

Eco-Schooling and Strategy Backing

Natural strategies and guidelines assume a critical part in tending to eco-challenges. Eco-training outfits people and networks with the information and apparatuses to take part in approach promotion. Educated and drawn in residents are better prepared to consider policymakers responsible and advocate for proof based natural guidelines.

For instance, eco-training plays had a critical impact in bringing issues to light about the significance of wetland protection. Wetlands, which give significant biological system administrations like water purging and flood control, are frequently compromised by advancement. Eco-training efforts advance the safeguarding of wetlands and empower promotion endeavors pointed toward reinforcing wetland insurance strategies.

Eco-Training and Youth Commitment

Drawing in youngsters in eco-training is fundamental for building a practical future. Youthful people are ready to acquire the natural difficulties we face today, making their association in eco-schooling basic. It imparts biological education since the beginning and enables youth to play a functioning job in ecological stewardship.

Drives like the Adolescent Environment Strike, drove by Greta Thunberg and a huge number of youthful activists all over the planet, epitomize the force of youth commitment in tending to the eco-challenge of environmental change. These developments raise worldwide mindfulness, call for guaranteed environment activity, and show the capability of informed and activated youth to drive change.

Eco-Training and Worldwide Joint effort

Numerous eco-challenges, for example, environmental change and biodiversity misfortune, rise above public boundaries. Worldwide coordinated effort is crucial for address these difficulties really. Eco-schooling encourages a worldwide viewpoint, advancing global collaboration and the sharing of best practices and information.

Endeavors like the Assembled Countries' Supportable Advancement Objectives (SDGs) represent the worldwide cooperation part of eco-training. The SDGs give a general structure to tending to a scope of eco-challenges, from destitution and yearning to clean water and environment activity. Eco-schooling is instrumental in bringing issues to light about the SDGs and assembling people and networks to add to their accomplishment.

Eco-Training Practically speaking

Eco-training isn't restricted to hypothetical information; it is best acknowledged through experiential learning and reasonable application. Nature-based encounters, field outings to environments, local area ventures, and involved exercises are vital to eco-training. These encounters cultivate a profound association with the climate and build up environmental ideas.

Eco-schools, for example, execute eco-training in educational programs and school works on, coordinating natural supportability into the day to day routines of understudies. They set out open doors for understudies to partake in natural drives, like reusing projects, planting, and energy preservation endeavors.

Chapter 4

Real-World Impact

Eco-mindfulness, driven by eco-training, fills in as the primary move toward tending to the multi-layered and squeezing eco-difficulties within recent memory. Be that as it may, the genuine proportion of progress lies in reality effect of the mindfulness raised. In this extensive conversation, we dive into the extraordinary capability of eco-mindfulness and its job in catalyzing substantial activities to alleviate, adjust to, and defeat the natural difficulties that pose a potential threat in the 21st 100 years.

The Force of Eco-Mindfulness

Eco-mindfulness, frequently produced through eco-schooling and natural missions, addresses the enlivening of cognizance about the natural issues that our planet faces. It reaches out past simple information; it incorporates a comprehension of the interdependencies of biological systems, the results of human activities, and the dire requirement for manageable practices. Eco-mindfulness is the impetus for a scope of ways of behaving and activities that all in all add to a more feasible and naturally cognizant society.

Eco-Mindfulness and Conduct Change

At the core of eco-mindfulness lies the potential for conduct change. Informed people are bound to take on naturally capable ways of behaving, like decreasing waste, moderating energy, and going with eco-cognizant customer decisions. Eco-mindfulness rouses activities that lessen one's biological impression, adding to the relief of eco-challenges.

Consider the decrease of single-use plastics to act as an illustration of how eco-mindfulness can drive conduct change. Expanded familiarity with the ecological outcomes of plastic waste, like its tirelessness in the climate and damage to natural life, has prompted a flood in buyer interest for choices and the reception of reusable items. Eco-mindfulness, for this situation, goes about as the catalyst for a huge decrease in plastic waste.

Eco-Mindfulness and Maintainable Ways of life

Eco-mindfulness is instrumental in the change to reasonable ways of life. It encourages a comprehensive way to deal with feasible living that goes past individual conduct change and reaches out to more extensive decisions in lodging, transportation, and food utilization. Manageable ways of life lessen the generally natural effect and add to the more extensive objectives of tending to eco-challenges.

The eco-challenge of urbanization, which frequently prompts the development of fabricated conditions to the detriment of normal scenes, is a region where eco-mindfulness can drive the reception of feasible residing rehearses. Metropolitan occupants, when had mindful of the effects of endless suburbia, may pick energy-productive lodging, advance public transportation, and backing green drives in their networks.

Eco-Mindfulness and Promotion

Eco-mindfulness stretches out past individual activities to incorporate aggregate endeavors and promotion. Educated and connected with residents are better prepared to consider policymakers responsible and advocate for earth dependable strategies and guidelines. Public help and support are significant in pushing for foundational changes that address eco-challenges really.

Environmental change is a perfect representation of how eco-mindfulness can fuel backing. Informed people and ecological associations advocate for aggressive environment approaches, like the decrease of ozone depleting substance emanations and interests in sustainable power. The worldwide youth environment development, exemplified by Greta Thunberg's Fridays for Future fights, outlines the capability of eco-attention to drive aggregate activity and impact strategy choices.

Eco-Mindfulness and Maintainable Utilization

Consumers decisions essentially affect eco-challenges, from environmental change to asset exhaustion. Eco-mindfulness impacts buying choices, empowering people to help eco-accommodating items and administrations. Besides, it cultivates an interest for straightforwardness and dependable strategic policies, at last driving business sector shifts towards maintainability.

Think about the shift towards reasonable and natural food items. Eco-mindfulness about the natural and wellbeing results of customary horticulture has prompted a developing interest for natural and privately obtained food sources. Accordingly, the food business has adjusted, offering a more extensive exhibit of ecologically cognizant items. This shift not just lessens the ecological effect of food creation yet additionally upholds feasible cultivating rehearses.

Eco-Mindfulness and Maintainable The travel industry

The travel industry, a significant worldwide industry, can have a huge ecological impression. Eco-mindfulness assumes a significant part in changing the travel industry area by advancing reasonable and dependable travel rehearses. Voyagers who are eco-mindful go with decisions that diminish the adverse consequences of the travel industry on environments, natural life, and nearby networks.

Eco-mindfulness with regards to the travel industry energizes practices, for example, ecotourism, which accentuates dependable travel to regular regions. Ecotourism advances protection, teaches explorers about neighborhood environments, and gives monetary advantages to nearby networks. It is a demonstration of how eco-mindfulness can cultivate supportable practices in a worldwide industry.

Eco-Mindfulness and Mechanical Development

Mechanical development and eco-mindfulness are characteristically connected. Eco-mindfulness encourages buyer interest for supportable advances as well as rouses creative answers for eco-challenges. Progresses in environmentally friendly power, supportable farming, and waste decrease are results of both eco-mindfulness and a guarantee to natural stewardship.

The improvement of electric vehicles (EVs) represents how eco-mindfulness drives mechanical development. As shoppers become progressively mindful of the ecological effect of customary gas fueled vehicles, the interest for EVs has developed. This, thus, has sped up the improvement of EV innovation and charging foundation, lessening ozone depleting substance emanations from the transportation area.

Eco-Mindfulness and Corporate Obligation

Organizations and companies assume a critical part in tending to eco-challenges. Eco-mindfulness energizes corporate obligation by encouraging straightforwardness, responsibility, and maintainability in strategic approaches. Informed customers and partners hold organizations to better expectations and advance moral and earth cognizant business choices.

The eco-challenge of plastic contamination gives an illustration of how eco-mindfulness can shape corporate obligation. As open consciousness of the hindering impacts of plastic waste has developed, many organizations have focused on lessening plastic bundling, embracing round economy standards, and putting resources into recyclable and biodegradable materials. This shift mirrors the impact of eco-mindful shoppers and their assumptions for dependable corporate way of behaving.

Eco-Mindfulness and Local area Commitment

Local area commitment is a strong result of eco-mindfulness. Informed people who know about eco-challenges and natural dangers frequently take part in local area drives, humanitarian effort, and neighborhood backing. These activities reinforce the securities inside networks and improve the aggregate reaction to eco-challenges.

Local area gardens, which are spaces where local area individuals develop food by and large, offer an illustration of how eco-mindfulness can cultivate local area commitment. Eco-mindful people who comprehend the natural and medical advantages of nearby, natural produce might decide to partake in or support local area gardens. These drives advance supportable food rehearses as well as cultivate a feeling of local area and shared liability.

Eco-Mindfulness and Youth Activism

Eco-mindfulness significantly affects youngsters, moving them to become dynamic members in tending to eco-challenges. Youth activism, typified by developments like the young environment strikes, addresses the force of eco-attention to prepare the future and induce change on a worldwide scale.

Greta Thunberg's Fridays for Future development, in which a huge number of youthful activists all over the planet request environment activity, outlines the groundbreaking capability of eco-mindfulness among youth. These developments have pushed environmental change to the very front of the worldwide plan and highlight the desperation of tending to this eco-challenge.

Eco-Mindfulness and Practical Administration

Eco-mindfulness illuminates residents about the significance regarding supportable administration and natural arrangements. In just social orders, informed electors are bound to help up-and-comers and arrangements that focus on natural security and address eco-challenges. The electing impact of eco-mindful residents can prompt political movements and a recharged obligation to natural stewardship.

For instance, the eco-mindfulness produced by the Rock water emergency in the US, which uncovered the risks of lead pollution in drinking water, filled public shock and prompted calls for further developed water foundation and more severe water quality guidelines. This emergency fills in as a sign of the force of eco-attention to consider states responsible and drive change.

Eco-Mindfulness and Natural Equity

Eco-mindfulness highlights the standards of natural equity. Understanding the variations in the natural effect of eco-challenges on weak networks, frequently because of financial elements, rouses people to advocate for fair arrangements. Natural equity is at the center of eco-mindfulness, directing activities that address variations and advance reasonableness.

The Standing Stone fights in the US, drove by the Standing Stone Sioux Clan and upheld by a worldwide alliance of natural activists, give a delineation of how eco-mindfulness can be bridled to advocate for natural equity. These fights went against the development of the Dakota Access Pipeline, which undermined the clan's water supply and consecrated lands.

4.1. The unique prize: spearheading environmental projects

In the fight against natural debasement and the approaching dangers of environmental change, leading ecological ventures addresses a special and strong system for tending to these squeezing difficulties. These undertakings offer a down to earth and noteworthy way to deal with moderating biological emergencies, rationing regular assets, and advancing feasible practices. In this thorough conversation, we dig into the meaning of ecological tasks and their capability to drive genuine change, embodying how committed people and associations can assume a critical part in safeguarding the climate and getting an economical future for all.

The Quintessence of Ecological Ventures

Natural ventures incorporate a wide exhibit of drives pointed toward resolving explicit environmental issues or more extensive maintainability objectives. They differ in scale, degree, and concentration, going from neighborhood local area driven endeavors to worldwide, enormous scope tries. These tasks try to address the diverse eco-challenges we face today, including environmental change, biodiversity misfortune, contamination, asset exhaustion, and territory debasement.

At the core of natural ventures lies the obligation to impact change and have a substantial effect on the planet. Whether driven by people, grassroots associations, companies, or legislatures, these tasks share a typical reason: to shield the climate, advance protection, and encourage economical practices.

Ecological Ventures: Impetuses for Change

Natural ventures are impetuses for change, filling in as a way to change over mindfulness and worry about environmental issues into substantial activities. They engage people and associations to channel their enthusiasm and responsibility into substantial, quantifiable outcomes. By tending to explicit natural difficulties, these activities add to the more extensive goals of supportability, environmental reclamation, and environment flexibility.

Consider the case of reforestation projects. Trees assume a fundamental part in moderating environmental change by engrossing carbon dioxide and giving fundamental living space to natural life. Reforestation drives center around establishing trees, frequently in regions where deforestation has happened. These tasks battle environmental change by sequestering carbon as well as further develop air and water quality and backing biodiversity.

Ecological Undertakings in real life: A Complex Methodology

Natural ventures take on a complex methodology, utilizing a blend of systems, instruments, and assets to accomplish their targets. This exhaustive methodology mirrors the complicated and interconnected nature of numerous eco-challenges. These tasks incorporate different exercises, for example,

Territory Rebuilding: Activities that attention on restoring biological systems, including wetlands, backwoods, and coral reefs, to reestablish natural equilibrium and backing biodiversity.

Reasonable Agribusiness: Drives that advance earth mindful cultivating rehearses, like natural horticulture, permaculture, and agroforestry, to diminish the ecological effect of food creation.

Environment Alleviation: Activities intended to lessen ozone depleting substance emanations through the reception of sustainable power, energy productivity, and carbon sequestration procedures.

Squander Decrease and Reusing: Endeavors to limit squander age and empower reusing, fertilizing the soil, and waste-to-energy arrangements.

Biodiversity Preservation: Drives pointed toward safeguarding imperiled species, protecting basic environments, and improving hereditary variety inside biological systems.

Local area Commitment: Undertakings that prepare networks and people to effectively take part in natural stewardship, training, and support.

Strategy and Backing: Drives that backer for ecologically dependable approaches and guidelines, elevating administrative change to resolve natural issues.

Corporate Supportability: Tasks attempted by organizations to decrease their natural impression through maintainable practices, green inventory chains, and mindful asset the executives.

True Instances of Natural Ventures

Natural tasks are not theoretical ideas; they are unmistakable and functional undertakings that have had a genuine effect. The accompanying models outline the variety and adequacy of natural activities across different eco-challenges:

1. **The Incomparable Green Wall:** A tremendous drive in Africa, the Incomparable Green Wall project looks to battle desertification and land debasement by establishing a mosaic of trees, bushes, and grasses across the Sahel locale. This undertaking addresses different eco-challenges, from land corruption to environmental change, and means to reestablish arable land, support neighborhood networks, and upgrade biodiversity.

2. **SolarAid:** SolarAid is a non-benefit association that works in Africa, attempting to give sun powered lighting to off-matrix networks. By conveying reasonable sun oriented lights and empowering sun powered business venture, SolarAid decreases energy neediness, mitigates fossil fuel byproducts, and works on the personal satisfaction for a great many individuals.

3. **The Sea Cleanup:** Established by Boyan Support, The Sea Cleanup project resolves the issue of sea plastic contamination by creating trend setting innovations to catch and eliminate plastic waste from the world's seas. Their imaginative framework uses latent drifting boundaries to think plastic trash for assortment, determined to tidy up 90% of drifting sea plastic.

4. **The Thousand years Seed Bank Association:** Drove by the Regal Botanic Nurseries, Kew, this drive centers around gathering, monitoring, and exploring seeds from wild plants around the world. The task shields plant variety, upholds biological system reclamation, and adds to worldwide food security by protecting hereditary assets.

5. **The Green Belt Venture:** Started by Nobel laureate Wangari Maathai, this local area based tree establishing project in Kenya looks to battle deforestation, soil disintegration, and advance local area strengthening. It embodies the force of grassroots endeavors in tending to natural difficulties.

These activities mirror the assorted techniques and approaches that can be utilized to address eco-challenges, from enormous scope worldwide drives to local area driven endeavors. They highlight the groundbreaking effect that committed people and associations can accomplish in the domain of ecological protection and supportability.

The Job of Ecological Tasks in Tending to Environmental Change

Environmental change, driven by the expansion in ozone harming substance outflows, is one of the most basic and pressing eco-challenges confronting the world. Ecological ventures assume a significant part in tending to environmental change through a scope of environment moderation and transformation techniques. These activities add to lessening discharges, upgrading environment versatility, and propelling the worldwide work to restrict temperature climb.

Environment Alleviation Activities

Environment alleviation projects intend to lessen ozone harming substance discharges, which are fundamentally answerable for an unnatural weather change. They envelop different procedures and activities, for example,

Sustainable power Drives: Undertakings that attention on the turn of events and reception of environmentally friendly power sources, including sun based, wind, and hydropower, to supplant petroleum derivatives and decrease fossil fuel byproducts.

Energy Effectiveness Projects: Endeavors to further develop energy proficiency in ventures, structures, and transportation, along these lines decreasing energy utilization and outflows.

Carbon Sequestration and Reforestation: Tasks that sequester carbon dioxide from the climate, like afforestation and reforestation, soil carbon capacity, and carbon catch and capacity (CCS) innovations.

Squander to-Energy Arrangements: Drives that convert natural waste into energy, for example, biogas creation from natural materials, lessening methane discharges and giving an environmentally friendly power source.

Low-Carbon Transportation: Activities that advance the utilization of electric vehicles, public transportation, cycling, and strolling, while at the same time upholding for strategies to decrease emanations from the transportation area.

Economical Horticulture: Endeavors to execute maintainable rural practices, for example, no-till cultivating, cover editing, and natural cultivating, which lessen fossil fuel byproducts from agribusiness.

Green Structure and Metropolitan Preparation: Tasks that underline energy-proficient and harmless to the ecosystem development rehearses, feasible metropolitan preparation, and green foundation to lessen discharges from structures and urban communities.

Environment Variation Tasks

Environment variation projects center around building versatility with the impacts of environmental change, including climbing temperatures, outrageous climate occasions, and ocean level ascent. These tasks address eco-challenges by:

Catastrophic event Readiness: Drives that improve readiness and reaction instruments for cataclysmic events, like flood guards, early admonition frameworks, and fiasco versatile foundation.

Environment Based Transformation: Ventures that utilization normal biological systems, similar to wetlands and mangroves, to give environment versatility and moderate the effect of environmental change on networks.

Water The executives: Endeavors to further develop water asset the board, for example, stormwater the board and reasonable water supply, to adapt to changing precipitation designs.

Horticultural Flexibility: Drives to foster dry spell safe yields, execute water-saving rural practices, and backing smallholder ranchers in adjusting to changing environment conditions.

Environment Versatile Foundation: Activities that retrofit and plan framework to endure environment related stressors, like strong scaffolds, seawalls, and transportation organizations.

4.2. Success stories of past winners

Throughout the long term, various people and associations have initiated natural tasks that address eco-challenges and add to an additional supportable and strong world. These examples of overcoming adversity act as motivating instances of what can be accomplished when committed people and gatherings channel their enthusiasm and responsibility right into it. In this far reaching investigation, we feature probably the most remarkable examples of overcoming adversity of past champs in the domain of ecological tasks, displaying their spearheading endeavors to safeguard the climate, advance preservation, and encourage feasible practices.

1. **Wangari Maathai - The Green Belt Task:**

   Wangari Maathai, a Kenyan earthy person and political extremist, is eminent for her exceptional work with the Green Belt Task. Established in 1977, this local area drove drive planned to battle deforestation, soil disintegration, and advance local area strengthening. The undertaking urged ladies to establish trees in their networks, tending to both environmental and social difficulties.

   The progress of the Green Belt Undertaking reached out a long ways past reforestation. It engaged ladies in Kenya by giving them potential open doors for money age and positions of authority. Wangari Maathai's vision reestablished scenes as well as prompted a more noteworthy consciousness of the relationship between environmental wellbeing and local area prosperity.

   Wangari Maathai's spearheading endeavors acquired her acknowledgment on the worldwide stage, including the Nobel Harmony Prize in 2004. Her work featured the groundbreaking capability of grassroots drives in tending to eco-challenges while further developing occupations and advancing orientation fairness.

2. **The Incomparable Green Wall - Fighting Desertification in Africa:**
   The Incomparable Green Wall project, started in Africa, is a titanic undertaking that expects to battle desertification and land debasement by establishing a mosaic of trees, bushes, and grasses across the Sahel district, spreading over from Senegal in the west to Djibouti in the east.

   This visionary undertaking addresses different eco-challenges, including land debasement, environmental change, and food security. By reestablishing arable land, the Incomparable Green Wall upholds neighborhood networks and upgrades biodiversity. It addresses a cooperative exertion, including north of 20 African nations and global accomplices.

   While the Incomparable Green Wall is a continuous undertaking, it has proactively gained huge headway in reestablishing biological systems and working on the vocations of millions of individuals in the Sahel district. It fills in as a demonstration of the groundbreaking effect of enormous scope, global endeavors to address eco-challenges and advance manageability.

3. **SolarAid - Giving Sun based Lighting in Africa:**
   SolarAid is a non-benefit association that works in Africa with the mission of giving sunlight based lighting to off-network networks. It was laid out to address energy destitution and lessen dependence on lamp fuel lights, which present wellbeing and ecological dangers.

   The association disperses reasonable sun based lights and empowers sun oriented business in African people group. These endeavors have not just superior the personal satisfaction for a great many individuals by giving admittance to perfect, dependable lighting yet have likewise decreased fossil fuel byproducts related with customary energy sources.

   SolarAid's work represents how admittance to clean energy can change lives, advance ecological supportability, and reduce the weight of energy neediness in underserved areas. The association's prosperity shows the potential for naturally cognizant drives to address both eco-difficulties and social imbalances.

4. **The Sea Cleanup - Handling Sea Plastic Contamination:**
   The Sea Cleanup, established by Boyan Support, is a weighty venture that spotlights on resolving the issue of sea plastic contamination. It created trend setting innovations to catch and eliminate plastic waste from the world's seas, especially enormous centralizations of plastic garbage tracked down in sea gyres.

   The Sea Cleanup's inventive framework utilizes uninvolved drifting obstructions to think plastic waste, making it more straightforward to gather and eliminate. By focusing on sea plastic contamination, the undertaking adds to safeguarding marine biological systems and the prosperity of beach front networks.

   This spearheading drive has gathered worldwide consideration and backing, displaying the capability of mechanical development in settling complex eco-challenges. The Sea Cleanup's work fills in as a convincing illustration of how a singular's commitment and creative reasoning can prompt extraordinary ecological arrangements.

5. **The Thousand years Seed Bank Association - Shielding Plant Variety:**
The Thousand years Seed Bank Organization, drove by the Illustrious Botanic Nurseries, Kew, is a worldwide drive that spotlights on gathering, rationing, and investigating seeds from wild plants around the world. The undertaking is committed to shielding plant variety and supporting biological rebuilding.

One of the venture's essential objectives is to protect hereditary assets, guaranteeing the accessibility of plant species for people in the future. This is especially fundamental for food security, biodiversity preservation, and biological system rebuilding.

The Thousand years Seed Bank Organization's prosperity lies in its obligation to preserving plant variety, advancing dependable seed assortment, and participating in cooperative endeavors around the world. By defending plant species, the task adds to biological flexibility and supports the drawn out soundness of our planet.

6. **Greta Thunberg and Fridays for Future - Youth Environment Activism:**
Greta Thunberg, a Swedish ecological dissident, earned worldwide respect for her part in motivating youth environment activism through the Fridays for Future development. The development started with Greta's performance fight outside the Swedish Parliament, requesting environment activity. Her single strike immediately developed into a worldwide youth-drove development.

Fridays for Future assembles youthful activists overall to request pressing environment activity from states and organizations. The development underlines the requirement for revolutionary changes to address environmental change and natural dangers successfully.

The effect of Greta Thunberg and Fridays for Future on environment strategies is significant. They have raised the direness of environment activity on the worldwide plan, rousing large number of youngsters to take part in fights and supporter for fundamental change. The development highlights the extraordinary capability of youth activism in tending to eco-challenges and advancing a practical future.

7. **The Worldwide Green Development Organization (GGGI) - Advancing Manageable Turn of events:**
The Worldwide Green Development Foundation (GGGI) is an intergovernmental association focused on advancing green development and maintainable turn of events. GGGI teams up with state run administrations and associations to progress ecologically capable financial development.

The progress of GGGI lies in its job as a facilitator and accomplice in the change to green economies. The association gives skill, specialized help, and strategy direction to help nations in their endeavors to accomplish economical and harmless to the ecosystem improvement.

GGGI's work exhibits the potential for worldwide cooperation and strategy backing to drive reasonable practices and address eco-challenges while cultivating monetary development.

8. **The Perfect Advancement Component (CDM) - Diminishing Emanations Through Tasks:**

The Spotless Advancement Instrument (CDM) is one of the adaptable systems laid out under the Kyoto Convention, pointed toward diminishing ozone harming substance emanations. It permits created nations to put resources into emanation decrease projects in non-industrial nations to balance their own outflows.

The CDM has been instrumental in advancing environmentally friendly power, energy productivity, and carbon sequestration projects around the world. By giving monetary impetuses to discharge decrease projects in emerging countries, it tends to environmental change and supports economical turn of events.

The CDM's prosperity lies in its capacity to channel monetary assets toward projects that moderate environmental change while advancing financial improvement in partaking nations.

9. **Preservation Worldwide - Safeguarding Biodiversity and Biological systems:**

Preservation Global is an association devoted to safeguarding biodiversity and biological systems around the world. Its work ranges from saving basic territories to advancing economical asset the board and pushing for protection strategies.

The association's prosperity lies in its extensive way to deal with preservation, which consolidates science, hands on work, and organizations with legislatures, neighborhood networks, and organizations. Protection Worldwide backings preservation endeavors in assorted biological systems, from tropical rainforests to marine conditions, and adds to the conservation of worldwide biodiversity.

These examples of overcoming adversity mirror the different and complex endeavors of people, associations, and developments in tending to eco-challenges and advancing maintainability. They highlight the extraordinary capability of devoted natural ventures and drives, showing the way that aggregate activity can have a significant effect in the world and its occupants.

4.3. The long-term effects of these projects on communities

Natural activities can possibly achieve significant and enduring changes in networks all over the planet. These tasks include a great many drives, from reforestation and clean energy reception to biodiversity protection and practical horticulture. Their drawn out consequences for networks are diverse, influencing monetary, social, and ecological aspects. In this far reaching investigation, we dive into the persevering through effects of natural undertakings on networks, revealing insight into how these drives address eco-challenges as well as encourage strength, work on personal satisfaction, and advance supportable practices.

Financial Maintainability and Vocations

One of the main long haul impacts of natural undertakings on networks is their commitment to monetary manageability and the improvement of occupations. These ventures frequently set out open doors for business, pay age, and monetary enhancement, especially in locales where conventional livelihoods might be ecologically impractical.

Work Creation: Ecological undertakings, for example, reforestation drives or the improvement of environmentally friendly power sources, habitually require a critical workforce. This occupation creation upholds the neighborhood economy and gives business open doors to local area individuals. For instance, tree establishing activities can utilize neighborhood inhabitants, decreasing joblessness rates.

Pay Age: As a rule, networks engaged with natural ventures can create pay through reasonable practices. This incorporates selling reasonably gathered timberland items, partaking in eco-the travel industry adventures, or delivering and selling environmentally friendly power.

Eco-Business venture: A few undertakings, similar to SolarAid's sunlight based light dissemination in Africa, support eco-business. This engages people to become business visionaries in the green economy, selling and circulating harmless to the ecosystem items and administrations.

Neighborhood Worth Chains: Ecological undertakings can animate nearby worth chains, supporting nearby organizations and cultivating financial confidence. Maintainable farming activities, for example, may advance nearby food creation and diminish reliance on imported merchandise.

These financial advantages reach out a long ways past the length of the actual ventures, establishing the groundwork for long haul monetary maintainability and independence inside networks.

Social Flexibility and Strengthening

Natural activities additionally add to social strength and local area strengthening. By connecting with networks in the dynamic cycle and building their ability, these ventures enable people and gatherings to play a functioning job in their own turn of events.

Natural Training: Many ventures consolidate ecological instruction, assisting local area individuals with grasping the significance of biological manageability. This schooling enables people to pursue informed choices and participate in eco-accommodating works on, cultivating a culture of natural stewardship.

Local area Preparation: Ecological ventures frequently activate networks, empowering them to meet up for a typical reason. This aggregate activity constructs a feeling of local area and fortifies social bonds, upgrading versatility despite challenges.

Administration and Support: Cooperation in ecological undertakings can develop nearby authority and promotion abilities. Local area pioneers frequently rise up out of these drives, pushing for dependable strategies and practices to protect the climate.

Orientation Strengthening: A few tasks, as Wangari Maathai's Green Belt Venture, enable ladies specifically by giving them pay creating open doors and influential positions. This orientation strengthening reaches out to different everyday issues, upgrading orientation equity.

Wellbeing and Prosperity: Further developed natural circumstances coming about because of these tasks can prompt better local area wellbeing and prosperity. Diminished air and water contamination, admittance to clean energy, and manageable food sources all add to better living.

Enabled and strong networks are better prepared to address eco-challenges as well as other cultural issues, guaranteeing enduring positive effects.

Ecological Protection and Strength

Maybe the most immediate and quick impact of natural tasks is the protection of biological systems and the advancement of environmental strength. Nonetheless, these impacts broaden into the future, offering networks a more steady and maintainable climate.

Biodiversity Protection: Many ventures center around biodiversity preservation and environment rebuilding. By securing and reestablishing environments, they assist with defending biodiversity for people in the future, safeguarding plant and creature species and their related biological system administrations.

Environment Versatility: Tending to environmental change is a focal point of various ecological undertakings. These drives, from reforestation to sustainable power reception, add to environment strength by sequestering carbon, decreasing outflows, and moderating environment related catastrophes.

Biological system Administrations: Sound environments offer fundamental types of assistance to networks, like clean air and water, fertilization, and flood control. Natural ventures secure and improve these administrations, guaranteeing a supportable progression of advantages into the indefinite future.

Normal Asset The executives: Supportable asset the board is basic for long haul biological versatility. Ecological ventures advance dependable practices that moderate assets, like water and timberlands, for people in the future.

The natural protection and flexibility encouraged by these undertakings lay the basis for a more steady and manageable future for networks.

Personal satisfaction and Prosperity

The drawn out impacts of natural tasks on networks are obvious in the superior personal satisfaction and generally speaking prosperity of local area individuals. These activities frequently lead to cleaner and better conditions, improving the day to day environments of occupants.

Further developed Air and Water Quality: Drives pointed toward lessening contamination and elevating supportable practices add to more readily air and water quality. Cleaner air and water lead to further developed wellbeing and prosperity for local area individuals.

Admittance to Clean Energy: Ventures that emphasis on environmentally friendly power reception furnish networks with admittance to perfect and solid energy sources. This lessens dependence on contaminating energizes as well as further develops energy access and security.

Nourishment and Food Security: Reasonable agribusiness projects upgrade food security by advancing neighborhood food creation and maintainable cultivating rehearses. This prompts better sustenance and decreased weakness to food deficiencies.

Strength to Cataclysmic events: Local area commitment in ecological ventures, like the improvement of calamity strong framework, upgrades versatility to catastrophic events. This converts into diminished dangers and better groundwork for outrageous occasions.

Social and Profound Association: Numerous ecological undertakings, especially those including living space rebuilding or the security of sacrosanct locales, fortify the social and otherworldly association of networks to their current circumstance. This association cultivates a feeling of character and prosperity.

Long haul Conduct Change and Manageability

Ecological ventures impact local area conduct and the maintainability of practices. The illustrations picked up during project execution frequently lead to supported eco-accommodating ways of behaving and rehearses in networks.

Social Change: Natural schooling and mindfulness crusades related with projects impart eco-accommodating ways of behaving in local area individuals. These ways of behaving frequently endure past the task's consummation.

Feasible Practices: Undertakings that advance reasonable practices, like natural cultivating or squander decrease, urge networks to embrace these pursues as long haul routines, diminishing their environmental impression.

Institutional Change: The outcome of ecological ventures can prompt institutional changes in networks, like the foundation of natural advisory groups or the consolidation of economical practices into nearby administration.

Eco-Business: In situations where eco-business is energized, local area individuals might keep on chasing after naturally dependable undertakings even after the task finishes up.

Difficulties and Contemplations

While the drawn out impacts of ecological ventures on networks are transcendently positive, there are difficulties and contemplations that should be recognized:

Manageability of Subsidizing: Many activities depend on outside financing, and supporting monetary help past the undertaking's life expectancy can challenge.

Networks should investigate roads for proceeded with monetary help or foster income creating exercises.

Changing Financial Setting: Monetary and social circumstances inside networks can change after some time, influencing the manageability of venture results. Adaptability and versatility are significant to address moving settings.

Observing and Assessment: Checking the drawn out effects of undertakings is fundamental to guarantee that they keep on helping networks. Vigorous observing and assessment systems are expected to follow progress.

Social and Social Contemplations: Social and social variables inside networks can impact the progress of activities. Perceiving and regarding these elements is indispensable for long haul project viability.

Strategy and Administrative Help: Tasks are frequently impacted by approaches and guidelines at neighborhood, provincial, and public levels. Proceeded with strategy support is important to keep up with project results.

Chapter 5

The Behind-the-Scenes

In the great embroidery of human life, there are in many cases stories and accounts that stay covered up, hid in the folds of history and eclipsed by additional unmistakable occasions. These accounts, the in the background stories, are the uncelebrated yet truly great individuals of our aggregate process. They are the stories that shape our reality in unpretentious yet significant ways, impacting our way of life, governmental issues, and society, in any event, when we know nothing about their reality.

One such in the background story is the job of ladies since the beginning of time. While history books are frequently loaded up with the adventures of men, ladies have assumed a fundamental however frequently unacknowledged part in molding our reality. Their commitments range from human expression and sciences to legislative issues and civil rights, and their accounts should be brought to the very front.

Ladies, from the beginning of time, have been the quiet draftsmen of progress. From the suffragettes who battled for ladies' on the right track to cast a ballot to the endless ladies who worked in production lines during The Second Great War, their effect has been significant. Ladies' support in the workforce during the conflict assumed a critical part in reshaping cultural standards, prompting more huge orientation fairness in the post-war years.

Be that as it may, ladies' commitments stretch out a long ways past the bounds of wartime manufacturing plants. Think about the universe of craftsmanship and writing, where ladies like Jane Austen, Virginia Woolf, and Frida Kahlo have left permanent imprints. Their work has improved our way of life as well as tested and reclassified conventional orientation jobs.

In science, ladies have made remarkable forward leaps. Rosalind Franklin's work in the early disclosure of the construction of DNA was instrumental, yet her commitments were much of the time eclipsed by her male partners, Watson and Cramp. Marie Curie, a trailblazer in the field of radioactivity, stays a symbol of female accomplishment in science. These ladies overcame cultural presumption and inclinations to make history.

In the background accounts likewise envelop the battle for social liberties and civil rights. Figures like Rosa Parks and Harriet Tubman, who assumed crucial parts in the American social liberties development, are praised today. Be that as it may, endless others toiled in haziness, pursuing similar objectives. Ladies' contribution in the social equality development was not restricted to the US; it was a worldwide peculiarity. Any semblance of Angela Davis and Audre Lorde made huge commitments to civil rights aims around the world.

These accounts uncover an example of ladies frequently working in the background to impact change. Numerous ladies from the beginning of time have confronted a twofold weight, shuffling cultural assumptions with their desires for individual and cultural progression. This mind boggling dance isn't restricted to one culture or period; a general encounter rises above overall setting.

This duality is especially obvious in governmental issues. Ladies have for quite some time been rejected from influential places, however they have reliably pushed for change. Figures like Eleanor Roosevelt and Golda Meir demonstrated that ladies could be powerful pioneers. The suffragette development of the mid twentieth century prepared for ladies' political cooperation, and today, ladies hold probably the most noteworthy workplaces in numerous nations. In any case, orientation differences persevere, and the excursion towards genuine orientation balance is continuous.

The effect of ladies in the labor force is obvious. Ladies have battled for their freedoms to work and acquire equivalent compensation, breaking obstructions in male-ruled fields. The tech business, for instance, has seen a rising number of ladies entering the field, testing generalizations and biases. Notwithstanding, ladies in tech keep on confronting separation and underrepresentation, featuring the work that still needs to be finished.

Additionally, ladies have been instrumental in molding worldwide economies. The job of ladies in the worldwide production network and agribusiness is frequently overlooked. From the ranchers who tend to harvests to the workers who collect items, ladies impact the worldwide economy. Ladies' monetary commitments are key to the turn of events and maintainability of numerous districts, and perceiving their work is vital for progressing financial equity.

The in the background accounts of ladies reach out into the domain of schooling. Since the beginning of time, ladies have battled for the option to learn, and their battles have prompted a more instructed and enabled female populace. Admittance to instruction is the way to orientation uniformity, and ladies like Malala Yousafzai and her devotion to young ladies' schooling represent the continuous fight for orientation balance around the world.

Furthermore, ladies have been fundamental in medical services and providing care. From Florence Songbird's spearheading work in nursing to the endless ladies who have filled in as guardians for their families, their commitments have been limitless.

Ladies' parts in medical care reach out to research and clinical leap forwards, however they are many times eclipsed by their male partners.

In the field of business, ladies have additionally been instrumental. The quantity of ladies possessed organizations has been consistently expanding, adding to financial development and variety. Be that as it may, ladies business visionaries keep on confronting special difficulties, from admittance to money to conquering generalizations. The tales of female business pioneers, as Oprah Winfrey and Sheryl Sandberg, motivate another age of ladies to break hindrances in the corporate world.

Ladies have been fundamental to social developments. The women's activist development, which arose in the nineteenth and twentieth hundreds of years, laid the foundation for contemporary conversations of orientation and sexuality. Figures like Gloria Steinem, Betty Friedan, and ringer snares have tested cultural standards and cultivated significant discussions about ladies' privileges.

In the domain of innovation, ladies have made critical commitments yet have frequently been disregarded. Ladies like Ada Lovelace, a nineteenth century mathematician thought about the world's most memorable software engineer, set up for current innovation. Today, ladies keep on making progress in the tech business, yet orientation differences continue, featuring the requirement for additional change.

Ladies' commitments to sports are additionally frequently underrated. Female competitors, from Billie Jean Lord to Serena Williams, have broken records and generalizations. Their achievements in the games world have progressed orientation balance as well as filled in as a motivation to little kids with dreams of athletic achievement.

The job of ladies in diversion is one more in the background story. Entertainers, chiefs, and makers have needed to explore a perplexing industry, testing assumptions and standards. Ladies like Meryl Streep and Kathryn Bigelow have made unmatched progress, separating obstructions for the ages that follow.

Ladies have likewise assumed a urgent part in ecological and maintainability developments. Figures like Rachel Carson, the creator of "Quiet Spring," started the advanced natural development with her work on the risks of pesticides. Ladies in native networks have been pioneers in feasible works on, protecting the climate for people in the future.

The effect of ladies in charity and social work couldn't possibly be more significant. Figures like Mother Teresa and Melinda Entryways have committed their lives to aiding the less lucky, having an effect on a worldwide scale. Ladies' commitment to worthy missions is a strong power for positive change.

The narratives of ladies in the military are frequently untold. Ladies have served in different limits since forever ago, from nursing on the forefronts to dynamic battle jobs. The commitments of ladies in the military have been fundamental for the safeguard of countries and the assurance of opportunities.

Notwithstanding these accomplishments, ladies play played crucial parts in logical leap forwards. Any semblance of Barbara McClintock, who reformed hereditary qualities research, and Jane Goodall, who changed how we might interpret primates, have made tremendous commitments to human information.

Another basic in the background story is the effect of ladies in religion. From the ones who have filled in as strict pioneers to the people who have tested orientation standards inside their confidence, their effect on strict organizations and practices is huge.

5.1. The making of an eco-warrior reality TV show

Unscripted tv has for quite some time been a staple of media outlets, giving watchers a brief look into the lives, difficulties, and wins of regular individuals. Throughout the long term, the class has developed to envelop a large number of subjects and subjects, from dating and cooking rivalries to endurance difficulties and ability challenges. In any case, one generally late pattern inside the unscripted television scene is the rise of projects revolved around environmentalism and eco-cognizant living. These shows plan to engage as well as teach watchers about the dire need to resolve natural issues. This story investigates the exceptional in the background excursion of making an eco-champion unscripted television show, revealing insight into the difficulties and possible effect of such an endeavor.

The idea of eco-cognizant unscripted television shows is established in the developing worldwide consciousness of natural issues, environmental change, and maintainability. As these worries have acquired conspicuousness out in the open talk, it is just normal that media outlets would mirror this shift by making shows that engage as well as move positive change. These shows plan to connect with watchers in significant discussions about the climate while advancing an economical way of life.

The principal critical stage in bringing an eco-hero unscripted television show to life is conceptualization. The show's makers should create a convincing and unique idea that spellbinds the crowd as well as lines up with the focal topic of environmentalism. The idea ought to preferably work out some kind of harmony among diversion and instruction, making it both connecting with and educational. It ought to likewise be engaging to the watchers, as the objective is to move them to make a move in their own lives.

One potential idea for an eco-hero unscripted television show could include competitors contending in a progression of eco-accommodating difficulties, like waste decrease, energy protection, and reasonable living. These difficulties could be intended to impersonate genuine situations, permitting the competitors to exhibit their obligation to the climate. The show's configuration could likewise consolidate components of cooperation, individual development, and mentorship, with laid out hippies directing and exhorting the challengers.

With the idea set up, the following stage is to get financing and sponsorship for the show. Natural unscripted television projects can be expensive to deliver, particularly assuming they include open air shoots, eco-accommodating difficulties, and specific specialists in the field. In this way, getting the help of earth cognizant backers and accomplices is fundamental. Organizations that are devoted to supportability and eco-accommodating items might see esteem in adjusting their image to a show that advances these qualities. Moreover, associations with natural charities or associations can assist with giving mastery and assets, upgrading the show's genuineness.

When the monetary and calculated perspectives are tended to, the projecting system starts. Finding the right challengers is critical to the progress of the show. Ideal competitors are energetic about natural issues as well as address different foundations, ages, and points of view. A blend of characters is fundamental to make convincing accounts and story circular segments that reverberate with watchers. The projecting group should likewise survey the candidates' obligation to having a constructive outcome on the climate, as the realness of their commitment is a center component of the show.

Eco-fighter unscripted television shows frequently highlight a different cast, with people who bring remarkable viewpoints and encounters connected with environmentalism. A few candidates might come from logical foundations, while others could have individual accounts of

conquering ecological difficulties in their lives. This variety adds profundity to the show as well as guarantees that different parts of environmentalism are covered, from preservation and sustainable power to practical farming and eco-accommodating innovation.

When the contenders are chosen, they are acquainted with the focal reason of the show, which regularly includes living in an earth cognizant local area or undertaking a progression of eco-challenges. The challengers should adjust to a way of life that limits their environmental impression, which frequently incorporates errands like waste decrease, water preservation, and dependable utilization. Their day to day routines are loaded up with eco-accommodating exercises, which can be both testing and educational.

The eco-challenges on the show are painstakingly intended to test the competitors' obligation to environmentalism and to instruct watchers about practical living. These difficulties might go from building eco-accommodating designs and developing their own food to directing natural life protection undertakings and creating environmentally friendly power arrangements. The candidates are contending with one another as well as pursuing a shared objective: to live as one with the climate.

A basic part of the show's prosperity is the direction given to the competitors. Master coaches and naturalists assume a critical part in the contenders' excursion, offering experiences, counsel, and pragmatic information. These tutors are much of the time unmistakable figures in the field of environmentalism, bringing an abundance of involvement and mastery to the show. Their job isn't just to teach yet additionally to move and persuade the contenders, encouraging a profound association with the ecological reason.

In the background, the creation group works eagerly to catch the contenders' encounters and difficulties. They utilize an assortment of shooting strategies, from customary cameras to drones, to catch the shocking scenes and eco-accommodating exercises. The cinematography is a fundamental part of the show, as it not just grand-stands the normal magnificence of the climate yet in addition passes on the message of ecological protection.

In the altering room, the recording is painstakingly created to make a convincing story. The objective is to engage as well as teach, and the altering system should find some kind of harmony between these two targets. The tales of the hopefuls' development, battles, and wins are woven together to connect with watchers genuinely and mentally. Moreover, the instructive parts of the show are improved through infographics, master interviews, and enlightening voiceovers.

The job of the show's host is additionally critical. The host fills in as an extension between the competitors and the watchers, directing the crowd through the eco-challenges, giving setting, and offering bits of knowledge. A charming and proficient host can essentially improve the watchers' association with the show and its message.

The profound and self-improvement of the hopefuls is a focal subject in numerous eco-champion unscripted television shows. As they face the difficulties and adjust to a maintainable way of life, watchers witness their change. This part of the show plans to rouse watchers to pursue eco-accommodating decisions in their own lives. It shows the way that anybody can set out on an excursion of positive change and have a tremendous effect on the climate.

A basic component of eco-champion unscripted television shows is the disposal cycle. In the same way as other reality rivalries, the competitors are slowly wiped out in view of their presentation and obligation to environmentalism. The end cycle adds a component of tension and show, keeping watchers drew in and put resources into the contenders' advancement. The end is much of the time done in a manner that underlines self-improvement and the opportunities for growth of the competitors, as opposed to simply zeroing in on rivalry.

The show's definitive victor not entirely set in stone by their general devotion to environmentalism and their capacity to rouse positive change in their own day to day routines and the existences of others. The champ might get a huge award, which could incorporate financing for an ecological task or the valuable chance to work with a natural association. This prize builds up the show's message that singular activities can significantly affect the climate.

Eco-fighter unscripted television shows are not without their difficulties and con-tentions. A few pundits contend that the configuration of unscripted tv can downplay significant ecological issues and misrepresent complex issues. They express worry that the cutthroat part of the shows might sabotage the earnestness of environmentalism and decrease it to simple amusement. Moreover, there is a gamble of "greenwashing," where the eco-accommodating picture of a show may not line up with its genuine natural effect, like the carbon impression of creation.

To address these worries, the makers and makers of eco-hero unscripted television shows should move toward the creation with a profound feeling of obligation. They ought to focus on credibility, exactness, and supportability in all parts of the show. This incorporates limiting the natural effect of creation, balancing fossil fuel byproducts, and working with specialists to guarantee that the eco-difficulties and way of life portrayed depend on sound environmental standards.

Eco-hero unscripted television shows likewise need to keep a harmony among diversion and training. While it is fundamental to connect with watchers, the emphasis ought to be on conveying the criticalness of ecological issues and motivating activity. This can be accomplished through well-informed content, drawing in narrating, and straightforward correspondence about the show's targets.

5.2. Insights from the show's creators and producers

The most common way of making an eco-champion unscripted television show includes a large group of difficulties and potential open doors, all of which rotate around the focal objective of drawing in and teaching crowds about environmentalism and reasonable living. The bits of knowledge and encounters of the show's makers and makers are essential in figuring out the elements of rejuvenating such a remarkable idea.

Conceptualization and Ideation:

The innovative strategy starts with conceptualizing and ideation, where the show's idea is conceived. As per the makers, one of the most basic viewpoints is creating an idea that is both engaging and instructive. The idea ought to reverberate with the crowd and move positive change. Finding some kind of harmony between the serious component of unscripted television and the more extensive message of environmentalism is fundamental. The makers stress that the idea ought to be established in true natural difficulties to keep up with legitimacy.

Monetary Contemplations and Sponsorships:

Getting financing and sponsorships is an essential move toward the show's creation. The expenses related with delivering an eco-champion unscripted television show can be significant, especially while calculating in eco-accommodating difficulties, master tutors, and shooting in different areas. Makers stress the significance of cooperating with earth cognizant supporters and associations that share the show's main goal. These organizations offer monetary help as well as offer aptitude and assets that might be of some value. Supports who are really devoted to supportability can likewise add to the show's validness.

Projecting and Variety:

The projecting system is a basic part of the show's prosperity. The makers and makers highlight the significance of choosing a different and drawing in gathering of competitors. These hopefuls shouldn't just be enthusiastic about ecological issues yet additionally come from various foundations, ages, and encounters. Variety among the competitors guarantees a scope of points of view and stories that can reverberate with a more extensive crowd. The determination cycle likewise considers the genuineness of the candidates' obligation to environmentalism.

Eco-Accommodating Difficulties:

The core of the show lies in the eco-accommodating difficulties that competitors face. The makers accentuate that these difficulties ought to be painstakingly intended to teach watchers about supportability while testing the competitors' commitment to the reason. These difficulties commonly envelop a great many exercises, like waste decrease, energy protection, and feasible living. They are organized to imitate genuine situations, empowering watchers to apply the illustrations learned in their own lives.

Master Guides:

The presence of master guides and earthy people is a significant component of the show. These coaches guide and exhort the candidates, sharing their broad information and experience. The makers and makers state that guides assume a fundamental part in cultivating a profound association between the contenders and the natural reason. They teach as well as rouse and propel, filling in as good examples for the candidates and watchers the same.

Shooting and Cinematography:

The visual part of the show is of most extreme significance. Makers depict how they utilize different shooting methods, from customary cameras to drones, to catch the stunning scenes and eco-accommodating exercises. The shocking visuals not just exhibit the normal excellence of the climate yet in addition assist with passing on the message of natural conservation. Cinematography is a strong instrument for drawing in the crowd genuinely and outwardly, upgrading the general effect of the show.

Account and Altering:

In the altering room, the crude film is carefully created into a convincing story. The makers and makers underline that the altering system is a sensitive harmony among diversion and instruction. The objective is to draw in watchers genuinely and mentally. The tales of the hopefuls' development, difficulties, and wins are woven together to make a story that resounds with the crowd. The altering system likewise consolidates infographics, master interviews, and useful voiceovers to upgrade the instructive parts of the show.

Host and Watcher Commitment:

The job of the host is critical in directing watchers through the eco-challenges, giving setting, and offering bits of knowledge. The makers and makers highlight the meaning of choosing a charming and learned have who can overcome any barrier between the hopefuls and the crowd. The host's capacity to connect with watchers is instrumental in passing on the show's message and rousing activity.

Self-improvement and Change:

A focal topic of numerous eco-hero unscripted television shows is the self-awareness and change of the hopefuls. Makers underscore that as contenders face the difficulties and adjust to an economical way of life, watchers witness their excursion. This part of the show means to move watchers to settle on eco-accommodating decisions in their own lives. It shows the way that anybody can set out on an excursion of positive change and have a huge effect on the climate.

Disposal Cycle:

In the same way as other reality rivalries, eco-champion unscripted television shows incorporate an end cycle. Candidates are continuously dispensed with in light of their exhibition and obligation to environmentalism. Makers feature that this cycle adds a component of tension and show, keeping watchers drew in and put resources into the hopefuls' advancement. Significantly, the disposal interaction is frequently intended to zero in on self-awareness and growth opportunities as opposed to simple rivalry.

Prize and Effect:

A definitive champ of the show is normally resolved in light of their general devotion to environmentalism and their capacity to rouse positive change. The makers and makers propose that the victor might get a huge award, for example, subsidizing for a natural venture or the valuable chance to work with an ecological association. This prize supports the show's message that singular activities can significantly affect the climate and urges watchers to make comparable strides.

Difficulties and Discussions:

The makers and makers recognize that there are difficulties and discussions related with eco-hero unscripted television shows. A few pundits contend that the configuration might minimize ecological issues or distort complex issues. It's vital for address these worries by guaranteeing that the show's substance is well-informed and precise. Furthermore, limiting the natural effect of creation and working with specialists to plan eco-accommodating moves assists with relieving these worries.

Obligation and Credibility:

To explore the difficulties and reactions, the makers and makers approach the creation with a profound feeling of obligation. They focus on credibility, precision, and manageability in all parts of the show. This incorporates limiting the natural effect of creation, balancing fossil fuel byproducts, and working with specialists to guarantee that the eco-difficulties and way of life portrayed depend on sound biological standards.

Adjusting Amusement and Instruction:

Adjusting diversion and training is a center goal of eco-hero unscripted television shows. The makers and makers underscore that while it is pivotal to connect with watchers, the essential spotlight ought to be on conveying the criticalness of ecological issues and rousing activity. This equilibrium is accomplished through well-informed content, drawing in narrating, and straightforward correspondence about the show's targets.

5.3. The challenges and ethical considerations in producing an eco-conscious show

Delivering an eco-cognizant show, whether it's an unscripted television program, narrative, or series revolved around environmentalism and manageability, accompanies an exceptional arrangement of difficulties and moral contemplations. While these shows intend to teach and motivate positive change, they should explore different obstacles to keep up with realness, maintain moral principles, and actually pass on their message. This story dives into the difficulties and moral contemplations related with creating eco-cognizant substance.

1. **Adjusting Diversion and Schooling:**
   One of the essential difficulties in making an eco-cognizant show is finding some kind of harmony among diversion and schooling. Makers should guarantee that the substance stays drawing in and enrapturing to draw in an expansive crowd. Simultaneously, the instructive part should not be compromised. Wandering excessively far towards unadulterated amusement could minimize serious natural issues, while inclining too intensely towards schooling might hinder watchers.

2. **Validness and Greenwashing:**
   Keeping up with validness is a focal moral thought in eco-cognizant substance. There is a gamble of greenwashing, where the show's eco-accommodating picture doesn't line up with its real natural effect. Watchers are progressively knowing and can distinguish unscrupulousness or inauthenticity. It's crucial for try to do is said others should do and show a certified obligation to natural causes. For instance, counterbalancing the carbon impression of creation and sticking to eco-accommodating guidelines are basic to keep away from charges of greenwashing.

3. **Portrayal and Variety:**
   Guaranteeing variety and portrayal in eco-cognizant shows isn't just a moral commitment yet in addition an imaginative test. These shows ought to mirror this present reality segment and social variety. An absence of portrayal can distance likely watchers and support generalizations. For instance, if an eco-cognizant show dominatingly highlights a particular segment, it might give the feeling that environmentalism is simply pertinent to that gathering.

4. **Monetary Requirements:**
   Delivering naturally engaged content can be costlier than conventional programming. Eco-accommodating practices, from involving manageable materials in set plan to limiting waste during shooting, frequently come at a higher cost than expected. These extra expenses can come down on the spending plan and require cautious intending to successfully apportion assets.

5. **Area and Travel:**
   Numerous eco-cognizant shows include going to different areas to film

eco-accommodating difficulties or feature normal magnificence. Heading out to remote or intriguing objections can present critical natural difficulties because of fossil fuel byproducts related with air travel. This moral situation is frequently settled by buying carbon counterbalances or carrying out eco-accommodating travel rehearses, however these actions could not totally invalidate the show's natural impression.

6. **Specialized and Creation Difficulties:**
Eco-cognizant shows frequently integrate progressed specialized components, for example, drones for elevated film and concentrated hardware for catching natural substance. These innovations might consume energy and assets, representing a test for keeping up with eco-accommodating principles during creation. Makers should search out economical other options or innovations with lower ecological effect.

7. **Moral Problem of Rivalry:**
In eco-cognizant unscripted television shows, the serious angle is key to the configuration. Contenders participate in difficulties, face ends, and compete for an award. The moral quandary emerges when rivalry eclipses the center message of environmentalism. Finding some kind of harmony among rivalry and natural training is quite difficult for makers. Guaranteeing that challengers' self-awareness and obligation to manageability overshadow contention is a sensitive errand.

8. **Long haul Effect and Way of life Changes:**
Eco-cognizant shows frequently portray hopefuls adjusting to manageable ways of life and eco-challenges over a moderately brief period. The moral inquiry is whether these progressions are feasible in the long haul or on the other hand on the off chance that they act as transitory changes for the show. Empowering durable changes and encouraging a profound obligation to environmentalism is fundamental to guarantee that the show's effect stretches out past its runtime.

9. **Moral Treatment of Hopefuls:**
Keeping up with moral treatment of hopefuls is a pivotal thought. The difficulties in eco-cognizant shows can be actually requesting and genuinely burdening. Makers should guarantee that the prosperity and wellbeing of candidates are focused on. Moral contemplations incorporate giving admittance to psychological well-being support, offering fair pay, and acquiring informed assent in regards to the idea of the difficulties.

10. **Straightforwardness and Trustworthiness:**
Straightforwardness and trustworthiness are moral goals while creating eco-cognizant substance. The show's makers and makers ought to be open about the means taken to limit the natural effect of creation. Straightforwardness additionally reaches out to portraying the two victories and disappointments in

eco-challenges, as well as this present reality hardships of embracing reasonable practices.

11. **Watcher Strengthening and Activity:**
The moral obligation of eco-cognizant shows goes past diversion and instruction. These shows expect to engage watchers to make a move in their own lives. Moral contemplations incorporate giving clear and reachable advances that watchers can take to have an effect in their networks and in the more extensive natural development.

12. **Staying away from Eco-Disgracing:**
Eco-cognizant shows ought to abstain from falling into the snare of eco-disgracing, where candidates or watchers are exposed to scorn or analysis for their past or current ways of behaving. The attention ought to be on empowering positive change and perceiving that everybody has space for development. Disgracing can be counterproductive and make protection from embracing maintainable practices.

13. **Mindful Item Situation and Sponsorships:**
Shows frequently depend on item situations and sponsorships to take care of expenses. A moral thought is guaranteeing that these items line up with the show's eco-accommodating qualities and don't advance impractical utilization. Makers ought to painstakingly assess sponsorships and associations to forestall any contentions with the show's ecological message.

14. **Moral Informing and Obligation to Science:**
The moral obligation to pass on exact logical data is vital. Eco-cognizant substance ought to be well-informed and in light of sound logical standards. Makers ought to stay away from embellishment or deception of natural issues, as this can disintegrate public confidence in the legitimacy of the message.

15. **Limiting Waste and Natural Effect:**
The eco-cognizant show's creation ought to be an illustration of the standards it advances. Limiting waste, lessening energy utilization, and embracing manageable practices in all parts of creation are fundamental moral contemplations. Makers should guarantee that the natural effect of creating the show is limited.

16. **Cultivating an Enduring Natural Effect:**

Eco-cognizant shows ought to go past bringing issues to light to cultivate an enduring natural effect. Moral contemplations remember the drawn out impacts of the show for watchers' way of behaving and the degree to which it motivates significant change. A definitive moral objective is to add to a more supportable and eco-cognizant world.

Chapter 6

The Environmental Issues

The world is right now confronting a bunch of squeezing natural issues that have extensive ramifications for the strength of our planet, the prosperity of its occupants, and the eventual fate of humankind. These issues are not separated issues but rather are interconnected and compound each other, making a perplexing snare of difficulties that request dire consideration and creative arrangements. In this conversation, we will investigate probably the most basic ecological issues confronting our planet today.

1. **Environmental Change and An Earth-wide temperature boost:**
   Environmental change is ostensibly the main ecological issue within recent memory. It is fundamentally determined by the expansion in ozone harming substance outflows, like carbon dioxide and methane, coming about because of human exercises, including the consuming of petroleum products, deforestation, and modern cycles. These gases trap heat in the World's climate, prompting climbing worldwide temperatures, a peculiarity known as an unnatural weather change. The outcomes of environmental change are expansive and incorporate more incessant and extreme climate occasions, ocean level ascent, upset biological systems, and dangers to food and water security. Tending to environmental change requires worldwide participation, progress to sustainable power sources, and far and wide protection endeavors.

2. **Biodiversity Misfortune and Species Elimination:**
   Biodiversity, the assortment of life on The planet, is under extreme danger because of living space annihilation, contamination, obtrusive species, and over-exploitation of regular assets. The outcome is a disturbing pace of species eradication, which upsets biological systems, lessens flexibility to ecological changes, and undermines the equilibrium of nature. Safeguarding
   biodiversity isn't simply an honest conviction; it is fundamental for the well-being of the planet. Preservation endeavors incorporate laying out safeguarded

regions, reasonable asset the board, and peaceful accords to forestall further loss of species and their territories.

3. **Deforestation and Environment Annihilation:**
Deforestation, the boundless getting free from timberlands for agribusiness, logging, and metropolitan turn of events, has huge natural and ecological results. Timberlands go about as carbon sinks, engrossing carbon dioxide from the air, and are home to a significant part of the world's biodiversity. The annihilation of these natural surroundings discharges put away carbon as well as compromises endless species. Reforestation, afforestation, and feasible ranger service rehearses are critical to relieve these issues.

4. **Sea Fermentation and Marine Biological system Decline:**
The world's seas are fundamental for directing the World's environment and supporting a different cluster of life. Notwithstanding, they are under danger from sea fermentation, fundamentally brought about by the ingestion of over-abundance carbon dioxide from the climate. As the seas become more acidic, it antagonistically affects marine life, especially on creatures with calcium carbonate shells, similar to corals and a few kinds of microscopic fish. This, thusly, upsets the whole marine pecking order, affecting fisheries and beach front economies. Lessening fossil fuel byproducts and safeguarding marine territories are fundamental for address this issue.

5. **Air Contamination and Unfortunate Air Quality:**
Air contamination, fundamentally coming about because of the consuming of non-renewable energy sources, modern cycles, and agrarian practices, adversely affects both human wellbeing and the climate. Particulate matter, ground-level ozone, and different contaminations can prompt respiratory sicknesses, cardiovascular issues, and, surprisingly, unexpected passing. Air contamination additionally adds to environmental change and influences biological systems by corrupting air and water quality. Executing cleaner advancements, working on open transportation, and moving to environmentally friendly power sources are imperative moves toward tending to air contamination.

6. **Water Contamination and Shortage:**
Water contamination, whether from modern releases, rural spillover, or inappropriate garbage removal, taints water sources, prompting an absence of safe drinking water and compromising sea-going environments. Notwithstanding contamination, expanding interest for water assets because of populace development and changing utilization designs has prompted water shortage in numerous districts. Maintainable water the board, contamination counteraction, and the preservation of freshwater biological systems are vital for address these difficulties.

7. **Plastic Contamination:**
The creation and ill-advised removal of single-use plastics have prompted a

worldwide emergency of plastic contamination. These materials persevere in the climate for many years, undermining untamed life, marine environments, and human wellbeing. Endeavors to decrease plastic contamination incorporate prohibiting single-use plastics, advancing reusing and practical bundling, and bringing issues to light about the significance of lessening plastic waste.

8. **Soil Corruption and Desertification:**
Soil corruption, brought about by variables like disintegration, supplement consumption, and deforestation, is a huge ecological issue that influences food security and adds to desertification. As arable land decreases, the world's ability to deliver food is under danger. Maintainable horticulture practices, afforestation, and soil protection are basic for fighting soil debasement and forestalling desertification.

9. **Overpopulation and Asset Consumption:**
Human overpopulation puts huge strain in the world's assets. The developing interest for food, water, energy, and land prompts asset exhaustion, natural debasement, and territory misfortune. Tending to overpopulation requires a mix of family arranging, schooling, and fair asset conveyance to guarantee a maintainable future for all.

10. **Squander The executives and Reusing:**
Legitimate waste administration is fundamental for forestalling contamination and the exhaustion of assets. Landfills, cremation, and ill-advised removal add to natural issues. Reusing, squander decrease, and reasonable waste administration rehearses are important to limit the natural effect of waste.

11. **Land Use and Urbanization:**
Urbanization and changes in land use bring about natural surroundings obliteration, deforestation, and soil debasement. Supportable metropolitan preparation, rewilding metropolitan regions, and safeguarding green spaces are fundamental for moderating the ecological results of land use changes.

12. **Regular Asset Exhaustion:**
The unreasonable extraction and utilization of regular assets, including minerals, non-renewable energy sources, and timberlands, exhaust these limited assets and add to ecological debasement. Progressing to environmentally friendly power sources, decreasing asset utilization, and advancing feasible asset the executives are key methodologies for tending to asset consumption.

13. **Food Creation and Agribusiness:**
Traditional agrarian works on, including the utilization of engineered pesticides, monoculture cultivating, and escalated animals creation, lead to soil corruption, water contamination, and biodiversity misfortune. Reasonable and regenerative agrarian techniques, like natural cultivating and agroecology, are crucial for guaranteeing food creation without compromising the climate.

14. **Outrageous Climate Occasions and Cataclysmic events:**
    The strengthening of environmental change prompts more successive and serious outrageous climate occasions, including storms, floods, out of control fires, and dry seasons. These occasions have expansive outcomes, from property harm to uprooting of networks. Readiness, debacle risk decrease, and world-wide environment activity are important to address the difficulties presented by outrageous climate occasions.
15. **Ecological Bad form and Variations:**

Ecological issues lopsidedly influence underestimated networks and low-pay populaces. These people group frequently endure the worst part of contamination, need admittance to clean water and sterilization, and are powerless against the impacts of environmental change. Tending to ecological shameful acts requires fair arrangements, local area strengthening, and comprehensive dynamic cycles.

6.1. Deep dive into the environmental challenges showcased on the show

A profound jump into the natural difficulties displayed on the show uncovers a large number of major problems that influence our planet. These difficulties act as a microcosm of the more extensive natural worries confronting mankind. In looking at them, we gain understanding into the complicated transaction of natural, social, and financial variables that underlie a considerable lot of the issues we experience in the cutting edge world.

1. **Environmental Change and A dangerous atmospheric deviation:**
   The show's portrayal of environmental change and a worldwide temperature alteration underscores the direness of this basic issue. The impacts of a warming planet are distinctively outlined through outrageous climate occasions, rising ocean levels, and the contracting of polar ice covers. Environmental change disturbs biological systems, imperils species, and undermines food and water security. The candidates' difficulties, intended to decrease their carbon impression and advance economical practices, feature the significance of making a move to relieve environmental change. The show shows the way that people can have an effect by taking on harmless to the ecosystem propensities and supporting strategies to lessen ozone depleting substance emanations.
2. **Biodiversity Misfortune and Species Termination:**
   Biodiversity misfortune is one more noticeable subject on the show. The difficulties frequently include the assurance of jeopardized species, preservation endeavors, and bringing issues to light about the significance of saving the planet's rich embroidery of life. The hopefuls' associations with different environments and untamed life highlight the delicacy of numerous species. The message is clear: biodiversity is pivotal for the strength of our planet, and we should go

to lengths to forestall species termination through territory protection, capable asset the board, and global participation.

3. **Deforestation and Living space Annihilation:**
The show's investigation of deforestation and living space annihilation brings issues to light about the results of far reaching backwoods clearing. Competitors might be entrusted with reforestation endeavors or upholding for mindful logging rehearses. The staggering effect of deforestation on carbon sequestration, nearby networks, and biodiversity is clearly depicted. The difficulties convey the significance of safeguarding timberlands and reestablishing corrupted scenes to alleviate ecological debasement.

4. **Sea Fermentation and Marine Biological system Decline:**
The show's emphasis on sea fermentation and the downfall of marine environments is an impactful indication of the interconnectedness of the World's frameworks. Competitors might participate in marine preservation projects, like coral reef rebuilding or marine species security. The results of sea fermentation, remembering coral fading and interruptions for the marine pecking order, are obviously portrayed. Watchers find out about the need of diminishing fossil fuel byproducts and saving marine environments to battle this basic issue.

5. **Plastic Contamination:**
The predominance of plastic contamination in the show features the universality of this ecological issue. Difficulties might include ocean side cleanups, diminishing plastic waste, and advancing capable shopper decisions. The visual effect of plastic waste on scenes, water bodies, and untamed life fills in as a distinct sign of the need to decrease single-use plastics, advance reusing, and change to practical bundling options. The show highlights the obligation of people and organizations to address plastic contamination.

6. **Air Contamination and Unfortunate Air Quality:**
Air contamination and its ramifications are one more major question investigated in the show. Hopefuls might be entrusted with drives to lessen air contamination in metropolitan regions, upholding for clean energy, and bringing issues to light about the wellbeing gambles related with unfortunate air quality. The difficulties uncover the unfriendly impacts of air contamination on human wellbeing and biological systems, underscoring the significance of changing to clean energy sources and further developing air quality through guidelines and economical practices.

7. **Water Contamination and Shortage:**
Water contamination and shortage are basic difficulties portrayed on the show. Competitors might participate in water protection, contamination anticipation, and support for clean water access. The results of water contamination, from tainted drinking water to upset amphibian environments, are capably conveyed.

The difficulties highlight the need of economical water the board, contamination anticipation, and fair admittance to clean water.

8. **Soil Corruption and Desertification:**
Soil corruption and desertification are ecological difficulties that frequently slip by everyone's notice, except the show points out these issues. Challengers might take part in soil preservation endeavors or tasks to battle desertification. The effects of soil disintegration, supplement exhaustion, and the deficiency of arable land are featured. The show conveys the meaning of maintainable farming practices, afforestation, and soil protection to battle soil corruption and forestall desertification.

9. **Overpopulation and Asset Exhaustion:**
The show investigates the difficulties related with overpopulation and asset exhaustion, despite the fact that it may not be basically as express as a few different issues. Hopefuls might take part in projects connected with economical asset the board and populace mindfulness. The message is clear: the developing interest for assets and the stresses in the world because of overpopulation require mindful asset utilization, fair conveyance, and family arranging drives.

10. **Land Use and Urbanization:**
Urbanization and changes in land use are analyzed with regards to ecological difficulties. Candidates might take part in manageable metropolitan arranging ventures or backer for green spaces. The difficulties stress the significance of dependable land use and metropolitan turn of events, including safeguarding green spaces and limiting the ecological effect of urbanization.

11. **Normal Asset Consumption:**
The exhaustion of regular assets is an inescapable issue featured on the show. Hopefuls might be associated with projects connected with maintainable asset extraction and dependable utilization. The difficulties highlight the criticalness of progressing to environmentally friendly power sources, decreasing asset utilization, and elevating reasonable asset the board to address this test.

12. **Food Creation and Agribusiness:**
Food creation and agribusiness are repeating topics in the show. Candidates might participate in agrarian maintainability projects, natural cultivating, and bringing issues to light about capable food decisions. The difficulties highlight the significance of feasible and regenerative farming practices, mindful domesticated animals the board, and the job of food creation in natural maintainability.

13. **Outrageous Climate Occasions and Cataclysmic events:**
The show additionally investigates the outcomes of outrageous climate occasions and catastrophic events. Contenders might take part in a debacle risk decrease drives, versatility building, and crisis reaction projects. The portrayal of typhoons, floods, fierce blazes, and different calamities fills in as a sign of the

requirement for readiness, transformation, and worldwide environment activity to address the difficulties presented by these occasions.

14. **Ecological Treachery and Abberations:**

The show addresses ecological shamefulness and variations, basically through hopefuls' connections with underestimated networks and weak populaces. Competitors might advocate for ecological equity and work on local area strengthening projects. The show accentuates the significance of fair strategies, local area incorporation, and addressing natural incongruities to accomplish economical arrangements.

6.2. Expert interviews on each issue

To acquire further experiences into the ecological difficulties exhibited on the show, we go to master interviews, where experts in each field give important points of view on the mind boggling main things.

Environmental Change and A worldwide temperature alteration:

Dr. Sarah Johnson, an environment researcher, features the squeezing idea of environmental change. She makes sense of that the warming of the Earth is essentially because of human exercises, stressing the job of ozone depleting substance emanations. Dr. Johnson focuses on that the outcomes of environmental change, like more regular and extreme climate occasions, can be moderated through the decrease of fossil fuel byproducts. She compliments the show's endeavors to bring issues to light about this basic issue and accepts that it assumes an imperative part in teaching people in general about the significance of making a move.

Biodiversity Misfortune and Species Annihilation:

Teacher David Mill operator, a prestigious scientist, examines the difficulties of biodiversity misfortune and species eradication. He calls attention to that human exercises, like deforestation and territory obliteration, are the essential drivers behind this issue. Teacher Mill operator underlines the significance of safeguarding environments, laying out safeguarded regions, and implementing protection measures. He praises the show's depiction of these difficulties, as it adds to raising public mindfulness about the need to safeguard imperiled species and protect environments.

Deforestation and Territory Obliteration:

Dr. Lisa Martinez, a specialist in ranger service and protection, makes sense of the meaning of deforestation and natural surroundings obliteration. She depicts how backwoods act as basic carbon sinks and give environments to a huge number of animal types. Dr. Martinez stresses the significance of mindful logging practices, reforestation, and the insurance of essential timberlands. She recognizes the show's attention on these issues, as it features the worldwide effect of deforestation and the requirement for feasible land use rehearses.

Sea Fermentation and Marine Biological system Decline:

Sea life researcher Dr. Michael Turner examines the difficulties of sea fermentation and the downfall of marine environments. He calls attention to that carbon dioxide retention by the seas is causing expanded corrosiveness, influencing coral reefs, marine species, and the whole marine pecking order. Dr. Turner underscores the need to lessen fossil fuel byproducts and safeguard marine living spaces. He applauds the show for revealing insight into these issues, as it brings issues to light about the inter-connectedness of the World's frameworks and the significance of safeguarding marine biological systems.

Plastic Contamination:

Natural extremist and marine preservationist, Lisa Chang, shares her aptitude on plastic contamination. She makes sense of the inescapable idea of plastic waste and its effect on the climate and natural life. Lisa advocates for the decrease of single-use plastics, further developed reusing rehearses, and the improvement of maintainable other options. She values the show's regard for plastic contamination, as it teaches watchers about the results of plastic waste and the significance of individual and aggregate activity.

Air Contamination and Unfortunate Air Quality:

Dr. James Anderson, a specialist in ecological wellbeing, digs into the difficulties of air contamination and its impacts on human wellbeing and environments. He features the job of modern outflows, transportation, and horticultural practices in adding to unfortunate air quality. Dr. Anderson underscores the requirement for clean energy sources, administrative measures, and public attention to address air contamination. He praises the show for resolving this issue, as it causes to notice the wellbeing gambles related with air contamination and the significance of decreasing emanations.

Water Contamination and Shortage:

Dr. Maria Rodriguez, a water asset subject matter expert, examines the difficulties of water contamination and shortage. She makes sense of how defilement from modern releases, horticultural spillover, and inappropriate garbage removal influences water sources and environments. Dr. Rodriguez stresses the significance of feasible water the executives, contamination avoidance, and evenhanded admittance to clean water. She lauds the show's depiction of these issues, as it instructs watchers about the significance of capable water use and the need to safeguard water assets.

Soil Debasement and Desertification:

Dr. Thomas Williams, a dirt researcher, gives bits of knowledge into the diffi-culties of soil debasement and desertification. He portrays how soil disintegration, supplement consumption, and deforestation lead to corrupted scenes and diminished horticultural efficiency. Dr. Williams underlines the significance of supportable agri-business practices, afforestation, and soil protection to battle these issues. He lauds the show for featuring the meaning of soil wellbeing and the requirement for dependable land use.

Overpopulation and Asset Exhaustion:

Populace master Dr. Emily Collins examines the difficulties of overpopulation and its effect on asset exhaustion. She makes sense of how the developing interest for assets strains the climate and prompts asset shortage. Dr. Collins advocates for family arranging, training, and fair asset appropriation. She values the show's depiction of overpopulation as it stresses the requirement for mindful populace development and asset utilization.

Land Use and Urbanization:

Metropolitan organizer and naturalist, Imprint Johnson, reveals insight into the difficulties of land use and urbanization. He makes sense of how quick urbanization can prompt natural surroundings annihilation, deforestation, and ecological corruption. Mark features the significance of economical metropolitan preparation, rewilding metropolitan regions, and safeguarding green spaces. He compliments the show for its consideration regarding dependable land use and the need to limit the natural effect of metropolitan turn of events.

Normal Asset Exhaustion:

Geologist and asset the executives master, Dr. Laura Evans, examines the difficulties of regular asset exhaustion. She portrays how the extreme extraction of minerals, petroleum derivatives, and woods drains limited assets and adds to ecological debasement. Dr. Evans advocates for environmentally friendly power sources, decreasing asset utilization, and feasible asset the executives. She values the show's emphasis on these issues, as it brings issues to light about the significance of progressing to maintainable assets and mindful utilization.

Food Creation and Horticulture:

Horticultural master and backer for feasible cultivating, John Smith, gives experiences into the difficulties of food creation and agribusiness. He makes sense of how regular cultivating rehearses, for example, engineered pesticides and monoculture cultivating, corrupt soil and mischief the climate. John advances reasonable and regenerative agrarian techniques, natural cultivating, and dependable domesticated animals the board. He applauds the show for its depiction of dependable food decisions and the job of maintainable agribusiness in natural preservation.

Outrageous Climate Occasions and Catastrophic events:

Dr. Emily White, an environment researcher work in outrageous climate occasions, examines the difficulties of catastrophic events and their strengthening because of environmental change. She makes sense of how tropical storms, floods, rapidly spreading fires, and dry spells have broad ramifications for networks and biological systems. Dr. White promoters for calamity risk decrease, readiness, and worldwide environment activity. She lauds the show for causing to notice the significance of tending to outrageous climate occasions and environmental change.

Natural Bad form and Inconsistencies:

Ecological equity advocate, Rachel Johnson, shares her bits of knowledge into the difficulties of natural shameful acts and inconsistencies. She features how minimized networks and low-pay populaces frequently endure the worst part of natural contamination and need admittance to clean assets. Rachel advocates for evenhanded strategies, local area strengthening, and comprehensive dynamic cycles. She values the show's depiction of these issues, as it underlines the significance of tending to ecological abberations and advancing equity in natural matters.

These master interviews give significant points of view on the natural difficulties exhibited on the show. The bits of knowledge from experts in each field highlight the intricacy and desperation of these issues and underscore the significance of informed activity, capable asset the board, and worldwide collaboration to address these basic difficulties and work toward an additional maintainable and versatile future.

6.3. The interconnectedness of these challenges

The ecological difficulties confronting our planet are not detached issues but rather are profoundly interconnected in a complicated trap of circumstances and logical results. These difficulties, whether connected with environmental change, biodiversity misfortune, contamination, or asset exhaustion, frequently fuel each other, making an outpouring of ecological issues with expansive ramifications for the soundness of our planet and its occupants. In this investigation, we dig into the complicated snare of interconnected ecological difficulties, understanding how they enhance each other and why comprehensive methodologies are fundamental for tending to them.

Environmental Change and A dangerous atmospheric devation:

Environmental change is the key part in the snare of interconnected natural difficulties. The emanation of ozone harming substances, essentially carbon dioxide and methane, is a key driver of an Earth-wide temperature boost. These gases trap heat in the World's climate, prompting an expansion in worldwide temperatures. The outcomes of environmental change swell across various other ecological difficulties:

Biodiversity Misfortune and Species Elimination: Increasing temperatures disturb biological systems, adjusting the natural surroundings and movement examples of innumerable species. Many battle to adjust and confront increased dangers of eradication.

Deforestation and Natural surroundings Obliteration: As temperatures climb, environments and backwoods are progressively defenseless against fierce blazes and nuisances, prompting deforestation. On the other hand, deforestation adds to environmental change by delivering put away carbon into the climate.

Sea Fermentation and Marine Biological system Decline: Warming oceans influence marine life, including coral reefs, while carbon dioxide is consumed by the seas, causing fermentation. Fermentation, thusly, influences marine species, especially those with calcium carbonate shells, and upsets the marine pecking order.

Air Contamination and Unfortunate Air Quality: Environmental change can heighten air contamination as higher temperatures lead to the development of ground-level ozone, a significant air poison. Outrageous intensity occasions and out of control fires likewise discharge air poisons.

Water Contamination and Shortage: Changes in temperature designs influence the accessibility and nature of water assets. Environment actuated dry spells and floods lead to water shortage and tainting, which compound water contamination challenges.

Plastic Contamination: The results of environmental change can be straightforwardly connected to plastic contamination. For example, more continuous and extreme tempests can prompt the dispersal of plastic waste into seas and streams.

Soil Debasement and Desertification: Modified precipitation designs and delayed dry spells coming about because of environmental change add to soil corruption and desertification, delivering land barren and inefficient.

Overpopulation and Asset Consumption: The effects of environmental change, like outrageous climate occasions and asset shortage, lopsidedly influence weak populaces and can drive movement and asset clashes.

Land Use and Urbanization: The development of metropolitan regions and changes in land use frequently ignore the weakness of environments and territories. Metropolitan intensity islands compound temperature expansions in urban communities.

Regular Asset Exhaustion: Environmental change strengthens the strain on normal assets, like freshwater, as it influences precipitation designs, adding to asset consumption.

Food Creation and Farming: Environmental change upsets rural examples, prompting crop disappointments, decreased yields, and difficulties in food creation.

Outrageous Climate Occasions and Catastrophic events: Environmental change escalates the recurrence and seriousness of outrageous climate occasions, including storms, floods, and rapidly spreading fires. These occasions significantly affect networks, environments, and assets.

Natural Unfairness and Differences: Weak people group are excessively impacted by the outcomes of environmental change, encountering an absence of admittance to assets and enduring the worst part of ecological treacheries.

The interconnectedness of environmental change with these ecological difficulties features the earnestness of tending to it as a focal mainstay of natural protection endeavors. Successful environmental change relief techniques can yield a huge number of advantages, from safeguarding biodiversity to diminishing air and water contamination and advancing supportable asset the board.

Biodiversity Misfortune and Species Elimination:

Biodiversity misfortune is naturally connected to environment annihilation, overexploitation of assets, and environmental change. The termination of species upsets biological systems and debilitates their capacity to adjust to ecological changes. This disturbance, thusly, enhances a few different difficulties:

Deforestation and Territory Annihilation: The obliteration of natural surroundings straightforwardly prompts biodiversity misfortune, as biological systems are supplanted by human foundation and agribusiness.

Sea Fermentation and Marine Biological system Decline: Biodiversity misfortune influences marine environments as different species assume basic parts in keeping up with the equilibrium of marine pecking orders.

Air Contamination and Unfortunate Air Quality: Loss of biodiversity can prompt lopsided characteristics in biological systems, expanding the gamble of air contamination through the aggregation of poisons.

Water Contamination and Shortage: Biodiversity adds to water refinement processes, and its misfortune can prompt water contamination and a decrease in the nature of oceanic environments.

Overpopulation and Asset Consumption: Asset concentrated overpopulation speeds up biodiversity misfortune through environment annihilation and overexploitation.

Land Use and Urbanization: The extension of metropolitan regions frequently prompts environment annihilation and discontinuity, further compounding biodiversity misfortune.

Food Creation and Agribusiness: Traditional farming practices can debase soil, add to the deficiency of biodiversity, and disturb biological systems.

Ecological Unfairness and Variations: Underestimated people group frequently endure the worst part of biodiversity misfortune, as they depend on regular assets for their jobs.

Tending to biodiversity misfortune and species annihilation is pivotal for biological system strength and flexibility, which, thus, can assist with moderating other natural difficulties.

Deforestation and Natural surroundings Annihilation:

Deforestation and natural surroundings obliteration are both a result and a reason for a few ecological difficulties. The outcomes of these exercises echo through the interconnected snare of difficulties:

Sea Fermentation and Marine Environment Decline: Deforestation and natural surroundings annihilation add to soil disintegration, which prompts the arrival of dregs into streams and, eventually, the sea. This sedimentation upsets marine biological systems and adds to sea fermentation.

Plastic Contamination: Clearing land for horticulture, logging, or metropolitan improvement frequently includes the utilization of plastic materials, which can add to plastic contamination through ill-advised removal.

Soil Debasement and Desertification: Land clearing is a significant driver of soil corruption, as it opens soil to disintegration and supplement exhaustion. This adds to desertification, delivering the land fruitless.

Overpopulation and Asset Exhaustion: The requirement for land and assets to help developing populaces frequently prompts deforestation and territory annihilation.

Land Use and Urbanization: The development of metropolitan regions frequently brings about the leeway of normal environments, prompting living space obliteration and biological disturbance.

Regular Asset Consumption: Deforestation adds to asset exhaustion, especially on account of lumber and non-sustainable assets.

Tending to deforestation and territory annihilation is fundamental for rationing biodiversity, safeguarding biological systems, and moderating the outcomes of soil debasement and desertification.

Sea Fermentation and Marine Biological system Decline:

Sea fermentation and the downfall of marine biological systems, essentially determined by the retention of carbon dioxide, have significant ramifications for the interconnected snare of ecological difficulties:

Plastic Contamination: Debilitating marine environments and coral reefs can prompt the amassing of plastic contamination as biological systems lose their ability to channel and oversee squander.

Air Contamination and Unfortunate Air Quality: The decay of marine environments influences the planet's oxygen and carbon dioxide trade, which has suggestions for air quality.

Soil Debasement and Desertification: Sea fermentation and its effect on marine environments can disturb the worldwide carbon cycle, which, thus, influences soil and land corruption.

Tending to sea fermentation and the decay of marine environments is crucial for protecting marine biodiversity, defending fisheries, and keeping up with the equilibrium of the World's frameworks.

Plastic Contamination:

Plastic contamination is both a direct natural test and a side effect of more extensive interconnected issues. Its belongings overflow through the ecological difficulties:

Air Contamination and Unfortunate Air Quality: Plastic waste, when burned, discharges harmful air poisons and intensifies unfortunate air quality.

Water Contamination and Shortage: Plastics, when separated into microplastics, can pollute water bodies, hurting amphibian environments and undermining water assets.

Soil Corruption and Desertification: Plastics, when discarded inappropriately, can debase soil quality, worsening soil debasement and desertification.

Overpopulation and Asset Exhaustion: The creation and utilization of single-use plastics are much of the time asset concentrated and add to asset consumption.

Land Use and Urbanization: The extension of metropolitan regions frequently prompts expanded utilization of plastic items and, hence, adds to plastic contamination.

Tending to plastic contamination includes squander the board as well as the more extensive difficulties of asset utilization, contamination counteraction, and supportable practices.

Chapter 7

The Contestants' Journey

In the immense and consistently developing scene of rivalry, where yearnings and dreams slam into crude assurance and ability, the excursion of hopefuls sets out on a wild and eccentric way. Whether it's in the domain of sports, expressions, diversion, or some other cutthroat field, the competitors' process is a microcosm of human life. It's an excursion loaded up with difficulties, ups and downs, penances, and at last, the quest for greatness.

At the core of any rivalry, there lies the person. The candidates, who could be competitors, performers, entertainers, or even experts in fields like math and science, all offer a typical characteristic - the tenacious quest for progress. This pursuit is many times conceived out of an energy, a passionate longing to succeed, to be awesome, to stretch the boundaries of human potential. They are the ones who hope against hope and set out to battle for those fantasies.

The excursion of these contenders regularly starts with a flash, an early interest or inclination for their picked field. This underlying interest shows them a way of investigation and self-disclosure. For some's purposes, it's an adoration for the vibe of a ball in their grasp, for other people, it's the agreeable reverberation of a melodic note, and for still others, it's the excitement of tackling complex conditions. Whatever the wellspring of their energy, this underlying association lights the fire of contest inside them.

As they dive further into their picked field, the candidates face the difficulties of leveling up their abilities and fostering their art. This period of the excursion is set apart by innumerable long stretches of training and learning. Competitors train determinedly, performers practice their instruments until their fingers hurt, and researchers dig into the complexities of their picked discipline. It's a period of devotion and assurance, where ability meets difficult work.

All through this excursion, the contenders are frequently stood up to with a decision - to endure or to surrender. The way to greatness is seldom a straight and smooth one. It's set apart by misfortunes, disappointments, and snapshots of uncertainty. These are the times when the genuine person of a challenger is tried. It's at these times that they should track down the inward solidarity to get themselves and continue onward. It's at these times that the fantasy turns into a main impetus, an encouraging sign that guides them through the obscurity.

The way of a contender isn't just about individual exertion. It's not unexpected an excursion that needs the help and conviction of people around them. Mentors, guides, and educators assume a pivotal part in molding the challengers' excursion. They give direction, intelligence, and some assistance when required. They see potential where others may not and assist with supporting it. They become something other than educators; they become coaches and now and again even substitute guardians, directing their proteges towards progress.

Notwithstanding tutors, loved ones likewise assume a huge part in the contenders' excursion. Their help, both close to home and monetary, is many times the foundation of a candidate's interest. The penances made by guardians, kin, and friends and family are incomprehensible. The excursion turns into an aggregate exertion, a common dream that everybody is put resources into. This encouraging group of people is the wellbeing net that permits candidates to face challenges, to push their limits, and to put stock in themselves.

As the hopefuls proceed with their excursion, they face the unavoidable difficulties of contest. It's here that they encounter their companions, their opponents, and the benchmarks of greatness. The opposition can be furious, and the tension monstrous. It's at these times that the challengers should not just depend on their ability and difficult work yet additionally on their psychological strength. The capacity to keep on track, to resist the urge to panic under tension, and to perform when it makes the biggest difference is a central trait of an effective challenger.

For competitors, the stage might be the Olympics, the World Cup, or the Super Bowl. For performers, it very well may be the great show lobby, or maybe an ability show on TV. Researchers might wind up vieing for lofty honors or examination awards. For each situation, the contenders should convey their best, frequently before a worldwide crowd. The heaviness of assumptions can be pulverizing, but on the other hand it makes their process so elating.

Progress in the realm of rivalry isn't just about ability and difficult work; it's likewise about versatility. The competitors should advance and enhance to remain on the ball. In sports, this could mean dominating new strategies or taking on state of the art preparing techniques. In artistic expression, it could include exploring different avenues regarding recent trends and pushing the limits of imagination. In science, it's tied in with remaining at the front of exploration and disclosure. The capacity to adjust and embrace change separates the bosses from the rest.

The contenders' process is frequently set apart by snapshots of brilliance and snapshots of hopelessness. They experience the happiness of triumph and the harshness of rout. These profound limits are a vital part of the cutthroat world. A gold decoration at the Olympics, a heartfelt applause at a show, or a leap forward in examination can unimaginably satisfy. Yet, they are likewise transitory minutes that are immediately supplanted by the quest for the following objective. Then again, misfortunes and disappointments can be squashing, prompting self-uncertainty and reflection. It's at these times of weakness that the contenders should track down the strength to return.

The idea of sportsmanship and fair play is one more fundamental part of the competitors' excursion. In our current reality where winning is everything, neglecting to focus on the qualities that genuinely matter is simple. Sportsmanship is about regard for one's adversaries, effortlessness in triumph, and pride in disgrace. It's tied in with playing the game with honesty and maintaining the soul of rivalry. Genuine bosses succeed in their field as well as act as good examples for other people, typifying the upsides of sportsmanship.

The excursion of challengers isn't simply an individual journey for greatness; it's likewise a wellspring of motivation for other people. Their accounts of assurance and strength act as inspiration for yearning people. At the point when a youthful competitor sees their good example win a gold decoration, or while a sprouting performer observes a virtuoso exhibition, it touches off a flash of trust and desire. The challengers become reference points of probability, demonstrating that fantasies can to be sure be transformed into reality through difficult work and devotion.

One of the surprising parts of the hopefuls' process is the feeling of local area that creates inside their particular fields. Whether it's a group of competitors, a gathering of performers, or an organization of researchers, there's a feeling of brotherhood and mutual perspective. Rivals on the field or stage frequently become companions off it. They figure out the penances and battles that accompany the quest for greatness. This feeling of local area is a wellspring of help and understanding, as well as an update that they are in good company in their excursion.

In the computerized age, the contenders' process is not generally bound to a nearby or public stage. It has turned into a worldwide peculiarity. Online entertainment, TV, and the web have changed the manner in which we see and follow rivalries. Competitors, specialists, and researchers are not generally known in the places where they grew up or nations; they have fans and devotees from around the world. This worldwide perceivability brings the two valuable open doors and difficulties. It implies that the all contenders' moves is investigated, yet it additionally opens up ways to new organizations and coordinated efforts.

7.1. Personal narratives and transformations

Human life is a mosaic of individual stories, a complicated transaction of encounters, decisions, and changes. Every individual's life is a special embroidery woven from strings of euphoria, distress, achievement, and disappointment. These individual stories are not only a narrative of occasions; they are an impression of the consistent course of change that characterizes our lives. In this investigation, we dive into the many-sided, in some cases turbulent, excursion of individual accounts and the significant changes that shape them.

At the core of each and every individual account is the person. We are the creators of our own accounts, the heroes in the stories of our lives. Our accounts start with the day we are conceived, and from that second forward, we become the storytellers of our own encounters. Our decisions, activities, and responses become the ink that composes the sections of our lives. As we cross the scene of presence, our stories develop, impacted by a huge number of variables.

Our initial years are set apart by the guiltlessness of young life. The principal stories are scratched in the straightforward delights of revelation and play. These are the narratives of our most memorable words, our initial steps, and the minutes when we initially perceive our general surroundings. As youngsters, we are both the makers and the essential crowd of these accounts. They shape how we might interpret the world and establish the groundwork for the stories that will follow.

Immaturity proclaims a time of fast change. It is a period of self-disclosure, prospering freedom, and the manufacturing of personality. Our accounts in this stage are loaded up with the disturbance of feelings, the adventure of first encounters, and the difficulties of growing up. We explore the moving territory of companionships, pounds, and the quest for dreams. The accounts of youthfulness mirror the growing identity, as we test the limits of our capacities and go up against the vulnerabilities representing things to come.

Quite possibly of the most groundbreaking experience that we as a whole experience is schooling. School is where our own stories become interwoven with the more extensive embroidered artwork of human information and culture. It is a position of scholarly development, self-disclosure, and the securing of abilities that will shape our fates. Our accounts in this setting are about scholarly accomplishments as well as about the connections we structure, the difficulties we survive, and the qualities we create.

Family, as well, assumes a focal part in our own stories. Our associations with guardians, kin, and more distant family individuals become complex strings that go through the embroidery of our lives. The stories of family are set apart by affection, backing, clashes, and the steadily advancing elements that shape our personalities. These accounts are frequently loaded down with feeling, mirroring the profound associations that tight spot us to those we hold dear.

As we move into adulthood, our own stories take on new aspects. We settle on decisions about schooling, vocations, and connections that will lastingly affect our lives. These stories are set apart by the quest for freedom and the journey for self-satisfaction. We put forth objectives, take a stab at progress, and stand up to difficulties that test our versatility and assurance. Our accounts in this period of life are much of the time a demonstration of our yearnings and the quest for satisfaction.

The stories of adoration and connections are the absolute most significant and extraordinary in our lives. Whether it's the tale of a first smash, the excursion of becoming hopelessly enamored, or the intricacies of long haul connections, these stories are an impression of our ability for weakness, sympathy, and development. Love can be a wellspring of satisfaction and satisfaction, yet it can likewise bring deplorability and significant change.

The accounts of misfortune and sorrow are an inescapable piece of the human experience. We as a whole face snapshots of torment, bitterness, and grieving. These accounts are set apart by the significant feelings that go with misfortune, as well as the versatility that empowers us to explore the profundities of pain and arise changed. Misfortune isn't simply a completion yet a start, an impetus for significant self-reflection and reconsideration of one's life.

The quest for dreams is one more subject that strings through our own stories. Whether it's a lifelong desire, an imaginative undertaking, or an individual objective, our accounts are much of the time set apart by the constancy with which we pursue our fantasies. The stories of desire are an impression of our vision for the future and the means we take to transform those fantasies into the real world. This excursion is loaded up sincerely, misfortunes, and at last, change.

Our accounts are individual as well as group. We are essential for networks, social orders, and societies that impact our own accounts. The accounts of society address issues of equity, uniformity, and the common human experience. Our singular accounts meet with these more extensive stories, affecting and being impacted by them. As we develop, we add to the continuous account of our times.

Individual changes can take many structures. They might be progressive, as we develop, learn, and adjust to new conditions. They may likewise be unexpected and significant, as we face life changing occasions, like sickness, misfortune, or an adjustment of individual conditions. These changes shape our characters and frequently lead us to rethink our qualities and needs. They push us to address what our identity is and who we need to turn into.

Notwithstanding misfortune, individual accounts frequently assume the topic of strength. We are tried by the difficulties life tosses our direction, and our stories mirror our capacity to quickly return, to track down strength even with trouble. The accounts of versatility are stories of conquering chances, of declining to be characterized by affliction, and of involving mishaps as venturing stones to more noteworthy levels.

Change is a steady in our lives, and the stories of progress are woven into the actual texture of our reality. Whether we pick change or it is pushed onto us, it requires flexibility and a readiness to relinquish the recognizable. The accounts of progress are frequently described by vulnerability, dread, and the expectation that goes with fresh starts. They mirror our capacity to embrace the obscure and to track down amazing open doors for development and change amidst change.

Individual accounts can likewise be profoundly impacted by the quest for reason and significance. Large numbers of us look for a more profound comprehension of ourselves and our spot on the planet. We set out on excursions of self-disclosure, frequently directed by contemplation, otherworldliness, or a quest for a more note-worthy reason. These stories mirror our journey for internal harmony, satisfaction, and the arrangement of our activities with our qualities.

Our relationship with time is a basic part of individual stories and changes. The stories of maturing and the progression of time are an indication of the fleetingness of life. As we become older, our viewpoints shift, and we frequently go through a reexamination of our needs and objectives. The stories of maturing are set apart by insight, acknowledgment, and a profound appreciation for the minutes that have molded us.

The computerized age has acquainted new aspects with our own stories. Virtual entertainment, online networks, and the multiplication of data have made it simpler to impart our accounts to a worldwide crowd. Our stories are not generally bound to the pages of journals or the discussions inside our nearby circles; they are currently apparent to the world. This perceivability has both positive and unfortunate results, as it offers open doors for association and self-articulation yet in addition presents difficulties connected with protection and validness.

The demonstration of sharing individual stories, whether through composition, craftsmanship, or different types of articulation, is an amazing asset for both self-disclosure and association with others. Through sharing our accounts, we make obligations of compassion and understanding. We find that our accounts, while novel, additionally contain general components that impact others. Along these lines, indi-vidual stories become a wellspring of motivation and an update that we are totally interconnected on this excursion of life.

7.2. Lessons learned along the way

Life is an unpredictable and always developing excursion, set apart by encounters that shape us and show us significant illustrations. As we explore the exciting bends in the road, we experience snapshots of euphoria and distress, achievement and dis-appointment, development and stagnation. Along this excursion, we assemble a gold mine of shrewdness that illuminates our comprehension regarding ourselves and our general surroundings. In this investigation, we dive into the examples advanced en route, the bits of knowledge that go with the embroidered artwork of our lives.

One of the earliest and most major examples we learn in life is the force of flexibility. From the second we make our most memorable strides and stagger, we start to com-prehend that disappointment isn't the end however a stage towards dominance. As youngsters, we fall, we scratch our knees, and we get back up, frequently with tears in our eyes. These early encounters instruct us that misfortunes are important for the excursion, and that by pushing through difficulty, we become more grounded and more competent.

Strength is an example that keeps on unfurling all through our lives. As we face the difficulties of immaturity, training, and vocation, we experience snapshots of disillusionment and dismissal. Whether it's a dismissal letter from a fantasy the everyday schedule bombed new employee screening, we discover that dismissal isn't an impression of our value however a redirection towards an alternate way. The capacity to return quickly from difficulties, to endure even with frustration, is an expertise that characterizes our ability for development.

Another illustration that rises up out of our life process is the significance of flexibility. Change is a consistent in our lives, and our capacity to embrace change and adjust to new conditions is a basic expertise. We discover that unbendingly clutching the past or opposing change can prompt stagnation. All things considered, we find that flexibility permits us to remain applicable, to track down new open doors, and to develop as people.

The illustration of versatility turns out to be especially impactful in the advanced age. The fast speed of innovative change and the interconnectedness of the worldwide world imply that we should constantly learn and adjust to new apparatuses, stages, and approaches to working. The capacity to embrace change isn't just an expert ability yet in addition an individual one. As we face shifts in connections, relational peculiarities, and life conditions, versatility empowers us to explore the intricacies of existence with elegance and strength.

Another significant illustration that rises up out of our process is the worth of sympathy. Our communications with others, whether they are outsiders or friends and family, uncover the force of understanding and empathy. Through sympathy, we figure out how to perceive the all inclusiveness of human encounters and feelings. We comprehend that everybody worries about their own concerns, fears, and dreams.

Compassion shows us the significance of tuning in, of really hearing the viewpoints and sensations of others. It welcomes us to step into another person's perspective and see the world from their vantage point. Compassion spans partitions, encourages association, and helps us to remember our common mankind. An example changes our connections as well as our capacity to have a constructive outcome on the planet.

The illustrations of sympathy and empathy additionally reach out to the domain of absolution. Along the way of life, we will undoubtedly experience snapshots of contention, hurt, and dissatisfaction in our connections. Figuring out how to excuse is an example that can be testing yet significantly freeing. Pardoning isn't tied in with approving horrendous acts yet about delivering the profound weight they convey.

The demonstration of absolution permits us to liberate ourselves from the heaviness of hatred and outrage. It is an example in giving up, in picking our own close to home prosperity over the longing for retaliation. Pardoning is a way to recuperating and harmony, both inside ourselves and in our connections. An illustration helps us to remember the groundbreaking force of effortlessness and the potential for recharging.

All through our excursion, we likewise come to perceive the example of appreciation. In the buzzing about of day to day existence, it is not difficult to zero in on what we need or what has turned out badly. In any case, appreciation helps us to move our point of view and recognize the overflow that encompasses us. It is the example of valuing the basic delights of life, the excellence of nature, the consideration of others, and the endowments we frequently underestimate.

Rehearsing appreciation is a strong method for developing an uplifting perspective and track down happiness right now. It advises us that joy isn't subject to outside conditions yet is an interior condition. The example of appreciation permits us to see the silver linings in testing circumstances and to encounter satisfaction in the conventional snapshots of life.

The excursion of life additionally shows us the example of using time productively and prioritization. In a world loaded up with vast interruptions and requests on our consideration, we should figure out how to really deal with our time. This illustration isn't just about efficiency; it is tied in with adjusting our activities to our qualities and objectives. About perceiving time is a limited asset and that what we decide to spend it significantly means for the nature of our lives.

Using time productively and prioritization frequently include defining limits, figuring out how to say no, and pursuing decisions that line up with our drawn out goals. It is an illustration in self-restraint and mindfulness. The capacity to focus on permits us to zero in on the main thing and to make a daily existence that mirrors our qualities and interests.

Perhaps of the most significant example advanced en route is the significance of confidence and self-acknowledgment. All through our excursion, we experience snapshots of self-question, self-analysis, and uncertainty. Nonetheless, we additionally discover that genuine self-esteem isn't dependent upon outer approval or flawlessness. Confidence instructs us that we are innately meriting affection and regard, similarly as we are.

Self-acknowledgment is the illustration of embracing our blemishes and defects, of perceiving that they are a fundamental piece of our uniqueness. It is an example in relinquishing the ridiculous norms and assumptions that we frequently force on ourselves. Self esteem and self-acknowledgment are the keys to inward harmony and bliss. They permit us to be kinder to ourselves and, thus, to stretch out that graciousness to other people.

The excursion of life is set apart by the example of self-revelation. We are ceaselessly developing, and with each experience, we gain a more profound comprehension of ourselves. We find our assets, our interests, and our motivation. Self-revelation is a continuous cycle that welcomes us to investigate our inclinations, our qualities, and the effect we need to make on the planet.

Self-disclosure frequently implies facing challenges and venturing outside our usual ranges of familiarity. An example requires contemplation and self-reflection. Through self-disclosure, we discover that our true capacity is endless, and that we are equipped for development and change all through our lives. An example welcomes us to ceaselessly look for our genuine selves and to live in arrangement with our actual qualities and goals.

As we venture through life, we additionally come to grasp the illustration of fleetingness. All that in life is dependent upon future developments, and nothing is long-lasting. This example can be a wellspring of both distress and freedom. It trains us to see the value in the excellence and worth of the current second, for it is temporary. It reminds us not to grip to connections or assumptions, as they are likely to change.

The illustration of temporariness welcomes us to relinquish the apprehension about misfortune and the requirement for control. It is an example in give up and acknowledgment of the normal patterns of life. Embracing fleetingness can be a way to more prominent inward harmony and the capacity to track down euphoria in the recurring pattern of life.

The excursion of life unfurls an example in the force of thoughtfulness and liberality. Thoughtful gestures, whether huge or little, have a gradually expanding influence that can contact the existences of others in significant ways. The example of generosity is tied in with perceiving the interconnectedness of every living being and the possibility to have a constructive outcome on the world.

Liberality is an example in giving, in material assets as well as in the endowment of time, consideration, and empathy. It is an example in perceiving that our activities have the ability to make positive change and to elevate those out of luck. Graciousness and liberality are demonstrations of noble cause as well as demonstrations of adoration, and they improve both the provider and the beneficiary.

The illustration of lowliness is another significant understanding that we gain on our life process. Lowliness instructs us that we are not faultless and that we are essential for a bigger entirety. It is an illustration in perceiving our own limits and the reliance of all life. Lowliness urges us to move toward existence with an open heart and a readiness to gain from others.

The illustration of modesty likewise includes an acknowledgment of the fleetingness of progress and the recurrent idea of life. It is an update that, regardless of how achieved we become, we are as yet powerless against the hardships of presence. Lowliness welcomes us to move toward progress with elegance and to stretch out a hand to the people who might be less lucky.

The excursion of life unfurls an example in the significance of chuckling and play. In the midst of the difficulties and obligations of adulthood, we discover that chuckling is a tonic for the spirit. The illustration of humor is an update that life ought not be made too much of, and that a funny bone can be a strong survival strategy despite difficulty.

Play is an example in reconnecting with the internal identity inside us. It is an update that life is intended to be delighted in, that we ought to set aside a few minutes for exercises that give pleasure and a feeling of immediacy. The examples of giggling and play add to our profound prosperity and assist us with tracking down balance amidst life's requests.

7.3. The impact on their lives after the show

Taking part in a TV program, whether it's a reality contest, an ability show, a television show, or some other classification, can be a groundbreaking encounter. Hopefuls who show up on such shows frequently wind up push into the spotlight, presented to new open doors, and confronted with interesting difficulties. The effect on their lives after the show can be significant, molding their vocations, connections, and self-awareness in manners they might not have expected.

For some competitors, the first and most quick effect of being on a TV program is the unexpected inundation of consideration and acknowledgment. Whether they become the victor or simply establish a huge connection, they end up in the public eye. Their recently discovered acclaim can bring both veneration and investigation. They could get fan mail and web-based entertainment adherents, yet they additionally become subject to popular sentiments, reactions, and, surprisingly, intrusive media inclusion.

This uplifted perceivability frequently prompts changes in their professions. Artists who perform well on ability shows, for instance, may get record arrangements and see their music contact a more extensive crowd. Entertainers and entertainers who earn respect on Programs might land more huge jobs in films or other TV series. Candidates with business thoughts might draw in financial backers or see their organizations develop quickly.

Be that as it may, the effect of TV openness on one's profession can be blended. While it can open entryways and set out open doors, it additionally puts huge tension on challengers to keep up with their prosperity. The abrupt ascent to distinction can be trying to explore, and the business' whimsicalness might prompt fast ascents and falls in ubiquity. Therefore, numerous contenders should be key in dealing with their professions present show on support and gain by their freshly discovered perceivability.

TV programs likewise bring critical monetary ramifications for competitors. The financial prizes can be significant for champs, frequently including monetary rewards and worthwhile agreements. Indeed, even non-champs can acquire significant totals through supports, public appearances, and authorizing bargains. These monetary open doors are prompt as well as lead to long haul pay and vocation steadiness.

Nonetheless, the monetary effect shifts generally founded on the idea of the show and the competitor's presentation. Not all hopefuls win significant awards or secure worthwhile arrangements, and some might confront monetary difficulties after their experience on TV. It is critical to perceive that media outlets can be eccentric, and challengers might have to painstakingly deal with their income to guarantee monetary steadiness past the show's term.

TV openness can likewise influence the individual existences of competitors. Associations with loved ones might advance as they wrestle with the challenger's freshly discovered notoriety and time responsibilities. A few contenders might find it trying to keep up with protection and a feeling of business as usual, as they become individuals of note continually under open examination.

Close connections can be especially impacted. The extraordinary timetable and tension of partaking in a TV program can strain special interactions. Then again, the freshly discovered distinction might draw in significant others who are keen on the hopeful's public persona as opposed to their actual self. Competitors should explore these intricacies and endeavor to keep up with legitimate connections in the midst of the progressions in their own lives.

One huge effect that reaches out past the network show is the impact on mental and close to home prosperity. The tension of rivalry, public investigation, and the requests of media outlets can negatively affect competitors' emotional well-being. The unexpected change from a confidential life to public life can be overpowering, prompting issues like nervousness, wretchedness, and even post-show "popularity burnout."

Competitors frequently face analysis and pessimistic remarks via online entertainment and in the press, which can be pernicious and sincerely burdening. Adapting to popularity, managing the strain to keep a public picture, and the frequently ridiculous assumptions can be a difficult part of life after the show. Challengers should focus on taking care of oneself, look for help from psychological well-being experts, and foster survival techniques to explore the profound effect.

One of the critical long haul effects of showing up on a TV program is the inheritance it makes. Challengers become piece of a bigger story, inside media outlets as well as according to general society. Their exhibitions, characters, and stories are scratched into the recollections of watchers. The inheritance can shape their future open doors and characterize how they are recalled.

A positive and significant heritage can prompt an enduring and fruitful profession in media outlets. It can furnish hopefuls with a dedicated fan base, underwriting arrangements, and potential open doors for future undertakings. Be that as it may, an ominous heritage can make it trying to push ahead in their vocations and may try and effect their own lives.

Candidates who have had their lives changed by a network show frequently become good examples and wellsprings of motivation. They can utilize their foundation to advocate for purposes they are enthusiastic about, bring issues to light of significant issues, and have a beneficial outcome on society. By utilizing their distinction for good, they can add to significant change and make an enduring and positive heritage.

A lesser-examined yet fundamental part of the effect of TV programs on challengers is the organization and connections they foster inside the business. Being essential for a network show gives candidates an interesting an open door to interface with compelling people, from makers and chiefs to individual challengers. These connections can prompt cooperative tasks, profession valuable open doors, and self-improvement.

Besides, the openness from a TV program can open ways to cooperation in different projects or appearances on television shows, reality side projects, or visitor jobs in famous series. The associations and encounters acquired during the underlying show can prompt a more different and dynamic profession in media outlets.

For certain hopefuls, support in a network show is a venturing stone to a long lasting vocation in the business. They might proceed to become regarded experts, even industry pioneers. The show can act as a platform, furnishing them with the acknowledgment and experience important to fabricate a long and fruitful profession. It is the establishment whereupon they can additionally foster their abilities and influence the amusement world.

TV programs likewise present open doors for self-improvement and self-revelation. The extraordinary rivalry, the criticism from judges or guides, and the difficulties looked by hopefuls can encourage flexibility, assurance, and a more profound comprehension of one's assets and shortcomings. These encounters become important life illustrations that stretch out past the show.

Candidates frequently consider how the excursion of partaking in a network show changed them, as experts as well as people. They figure out how to oversee pressure, handle analysis, and adjust to different conditions. These examples are adaptable and can be applied in different parts of their lives, from individual connections to future vocation tries.

www.ingramcontent.com/pod-product-compliance
Lightning Source LLC
LaVergne TN
LVHW020908200726
843506LV00011B/1615